Propellerhead Reason TIPS AND TRICKS

Hollin Jones

PC Publishing

PC Publishing
Keeper's House
Merton
Thetford
Norfolk IP25 6QH
UK

Tel 01953 889900
Fax 01953 889901
email info@pc-publishing.com
website http://www.pc-publishing.com

First published 2005
Reprinted 2006, 2007

ISBN 1 870775 97 X

British Library Cataloguing in Publication Data
A catalogue record for this book is available from the British Library

Cover design by Hilary Norman Design Ltd

Printed and bound in Great Britain by Cromwell Press, Trowbridge, Wilts

Preface

For a long time, sequencing music on computers was predominantly the domain of people who had enough technical knowledge to understand the intricacies of their software. The need to make sequencers user-friendly was not highest on the list of manufactuter's priorities. For beginners or those with an intermediate level of technical skill, hardware was usually the best way to build a recording setup. Tape machines, drum machines, keyboard workstations and hardware samplers were the order of the day.

As with so many aspects of modern life, the computer quickly and decisively took over in the mid to late 1990s. As computers got more powerful and less expensive, owning and running a computer-based studio became a realistic goal for anyone interested in making music. As this happened, software manufacturers began to realise the potential that this new market offered them. When Propellerhead Software released Reason, it revolutionised the way we thought about sequencers. Based on the idea of a real rack of instruments, Reason just made sense. Deciding not to incorporate audio recording features or VST support, Propellerhead focused instead on making Reason very stable, self-contained and easy to use. They succeeded in their aims, and Reason became incredibly popular with musicians worldwide.

Reason's main strength is that it is as simple or complex as you want to make it. Beginners can be making music within ten minutes of having installed it. Seasoned users can get much more out of it than you'd guess at first glance. And it is for all Reason users that this book has been written. Every piece of software has hidden tricks, timesaving shortcuts and surprising features, and Reason is no exception. From version 1 through 2 and now 3 it's seen some major additions, new instruments and effects and workflow improvements that make it a great tool for musicians of all levels. Each instrument and effect is covered, as well as general working methods, workflow tips and advice on using computers for music production. It isn't an exhaustive list of every feature of every module, but rather a guide to using Reason in real-world situations. Only by using the program can you uncover its hidden depths, and this book provides useful insider tips that will help you be more creative, work faster and work smarter with Reason.

Reason is cross-platform, and so almost all tips apply to both Windows and Mac versions. Where there are differences, they are clearly marked. Whether you read the book cover to cover or just when you need to know more about a specific part of working with Reason, you're sure to learn something new that makes your Reason experience even better.

Contents

Setting up

Before you start

Working with audio is one of the most power-intensive things a computer can be asked to do. As CPU speeds go up, so do our expectations of what we should be able to do with our machines. Luckily, Reason's system requirements are considerably lower than those of many other sequencers. This is partly because it is self-contained, and because of that the programmers can fine tune it for maximum performance, knowing it won't have to deal with external plugins or third-party effects. But even though the minimum system requirements are low, it's still highly advisable to get a powerful computer, preferably built specially for working with audio. An off-the-shelf PC might be OK but you'll find it may struggle with more intensive music projects. Here are some factors to consider when choosing a PC for audio work:

- Processor speed.
- Hard drive size
- RAM capacity
- Expansion options
- Fan noise

Whilst most new PCs would meet the minimum system requirements for Reason, there are a number of arguments for buying one with a better specification.

- The faster the CPU, the more effects and instruments you can run.
- A larger hard drive can store more data and helps modern operating systems to run better
- More RAM means better sample playback, and generally benefits the running of a computer.
- PCI and drive slots as well as USB and FireWire ports allow more flexibility to use audio and MIDI interfaces and add external hard drives
- A quieter computer is less likely to interfere with live recordings in other software such as Cubase.

Mac or PC

This is a long-running debate with evangelists on either side, but the sensible view is that both have their strengths and weaknesses. Increasingly for musicians your choice of platform is determined by your preferred sequencer. Logic, for example, is now Mac only. Sonar by contrast is PC only. Reason, happily, runs on either, and the feature set on both platforms is identical. Version 2.5 even still runs on Mac OS9, which is rare these days as the Mac world has mostly migrated to using OSX. A few studios have stuck with OS9 for various reasons, but OS9 support isn't present in version 3.

A quick comparison of Macs and PCs

Macs tend to be more expensive to buy initially, although prices have dropped considerably. The eMac as shown in Figure 1.1 represents a surprisingly cheap and

Figure 1.1
Apple's eMac is a low-cost but powerful entry-level system for running music applications.

Figure 1.2
The Mac Mini is a low-cost way to own a relatively powerful Mac

Figure 1.3
PCs can be built to order from various components. More choice, but to avoid pitfalls, use a pro audio PC specialist.

powerful entry-level Mac. Mac OSX tends to be very stable, but runs better on faster machines. When you buy a Mac you know that it has been built to a specification set by Apple, and so hardware / software conflicts are rare.   Peripherals often run without any additional drivers, and as an aside, Macs look good too!

Windows PCs are generally cheaper to buy, and building or buying one made of components you specify yourself is fairly straightforward. PC shops are found in every town, and Windows 2000 and XP are held to be "snappier" in general operation than Mac OSX. On the flipside, a PC is much more at the mercy of the drivers written for its components to allow them to talk to each other. A bad driver can mean hours spent on a helpline. Troubleshooting Windows can require a lot of technical knowledge, and it is prone to viruses, unlike the Mac.

A lot of people stick with what they know, and ultimately it's personal preference that will dictate your choice of platform. Luckily, Reason works well on both.

Installing Reason

On the Mac

Installation is fairly straightforward. Double clicking the installer icon runs you through the process. When installing Reason 2.5 on the Mac, choose Easy Install to install the Program, Factory and Orkester Sound Banks. Reason needs at least one sound bank present to work. If you don't install the Factory Bank now, it will ask for you to insert the CD every time you run the program. The Sound Banks take up around 530MB each, and have all the sounds you need to get started. If you don't want to install the sound banks, or are returning later to install a sound bank you omitted earlier, choose Custom Install. By checking or unchecking the boxes you can specify which to leave or include. If you just install the program at first, you can drag and drop the Sound Banks to your hard drive later. The other two CDs just contain these ReFills, and drag and drop works as well as using the installer.

If you are installing Reason 3 you will be prompted to insert the sound bank CDs on first install. You do not have the choice to install them later – the installer will not complete without them.

Where to go

From the installer you can select which drive to install the files to, if you have more than one hard drive. By clicking Select Folder you can choose a subfolder from a drive.

Figure 1.4
Choose where to install Reason and its sound banks on the Mac

On the PC

Windows 2000 and XP will probably autorun the Reason installer. If not, go to the start menu and select Run, then type d:/ or whatever the name of your optical drive is. Alternatively, go to My Computer > Program Disc. Then double click the Install Reason icon. It's a good idea to quit all other running programs before starting the installer.

Figure 1.5
The installation procedure is very easy on both platforms

Location, location

With Reason 2.5, Windows asks whether you want to install the Sound Banks, and if so, where. If for any reason you don't want to install them, or want to put them somewhere other than the default location, use the dropdown menus next to their names to specify this. In Reason 3, you have to install the sound banks at the time of installation. In fact there's no option to do this later.

Figure 1.6
Reason requires you to have the Sound Banks present. It's sensible to keep them in the Reason folder

Preferences

Reason's preferences determine how it interacts with your system and what settings it should use. They also let you tweak Reason for specific purposes and systems. The most important are the audio and MIDI settings, as they control how Reason receives and transmits all its data. Here is a look how best to set the preferences.

General

This, unsurprisingly, contains general settings for Reason's operation. The Appearance settings are a matter of personal choice, whether you want cables to animate and tooltips to appear. These are usually best left switched on.

    The default song option lets you specify what Reason should do when you boot it up each time. By default it opens an empty rack, a blank canvas for you to start with. Selecting Built In opens the standard Reason demo song – which is a bit pointless to have open every time you start it up. The most useful option here is to select Custom, and use the file browser button to navigate to a project file. Let's say you always or more often than not work with the same kind of setup. A typical example of this might be a mixer, some reverbs and compressors, a piano and some drums and a bass loaded into various modules. Rather than having to manually add these each time, create a template song with all the modules set up but no MIDI recorded, and save it as a file called something like basictemplate.rns. If you set Reason to open this file on startup you'll save time setting up a new rack every session.

    The CPU usage limit menu tells Reason at what point it should stop demanding more power from your processor. On a slower machine you may want to impose a limit, especially if

Figure 1.7
Specify a template song to load up when you start Reason

Figure 1.8
Making template files read-only.

Figure 1.9
On a decent machine, try leaving the CPU limiter effectively off

you are running other software alongside Reason, so that it doesn't drain the system too much. Limiting it to 80% of the CPU would ensure it left some capacity for the other programs. In reality though, Reason is much kinder to processors than many other sequencers. Even on a moderately powered machine you will be able to switch this setting to No Limit and not notice any adverse effects until projects get very large. As all processing is done in-house, (inside Reason) the programmers have been able to optimize it for maximum CPU efficiency. On a modern machine you can leave the High Resolution Samples option switched on as well, as it's unlikely to trouble your computer.

Audio

This is where you tell Reason which device to use to transmit sound. The Master Tune control will alter the main tuning setting for the whole program. In practice you'll almost certainly never need to use this. The great thing about computer sequencers is that you can be sure they're always in tune. The only reason to use

Figure 1.10
Choosing a sound output device

Tip

If you're just getting started and can't get any sound output, check that the program is set to use your sound card and isn't set to No Sound. Also check that your card drivers are up to date and that the volume is turned up.

this would be in a situation where you had to match a Reason track to other recorded material that had itself been recorded out of tune. Under the Audio Card setting you choose which device to use to fire sound out of Reason. In practice you'll probably only have one sound card active, and you should choose it from the list.

The Sample Rate option is based on the available rates supported by your soundcard. Low end cards will support up to 44.1kHz, higher spec ones up to 96kHz and some even up to 192kHz. As a rule of thumb, work at 44.1kHz, as this is CD quality. 48kHz is the standard for DAT and DVD but you can encounter issues when moving files to hardware with different capabilities. Usually this involves a track playing slower or quicker than it should for no apparent reason. The way around this is to resample the track to a sample rate supported by the new hardware. Equally, there's no real point in working at a sample rate of less than 44.1kHz unless you know why you need to.

Tip

Mac users – if you are having trouble getting sound output, switch the preferences to use Built In Audio. All Macs have an internal soundcard and at least one speaker as standard. If you can get sound out of the Mac speaker but not the third-party soundcard, the problem isn't with Reason but with the settings of the other card. On PC or Mac you can always try plugging headphones into the built-in soundcard to test where a fault is occurring.

Figure 1.11
Even though some very high sample rates may be available, you don't normally need them

The buffer settings control the streaming of audio between software and hardware. Buffer size is important because it affects the latency of MIDI and the reliability of audio playback. Latency is a small but annoying gap between your pressing a key and hearing the sound. Too much latency can make it impossible to play in time. Setting a lower buffer size reduces the latency but also increases the risk of pops and clicks in the audio playback. Raising the buffer size increases latency but makes for improved audio performance. As all hardware setups are different there's no strict rule for what setting to use, although a buffer size of 256 or 512 samples is often a good bet. Experiment with settings to see what works best and gives you minimum latency but maximum audio quality.

Tip

Here's a good rule of thumb : when you're playing MIDI in a lot and writing music, use a lower buffer setting to get minimum latency. Then when you're arranging and mixing, increase the buffer size to improve audio performance. If you're not playing in any more the latency won't be an issue.

Figure 1.12
Lower buffer settings for lower latency

Reason supports up to 64 channels of audio output. You can see them on the Audio Out module at the top of the rack. If your audio interface supports more than two output channels, you can activate them in the audio preferences box and connect instruments or mixers to them. Sound will then be routed to the hardware outputs on your interface as you decide in the preferences,

Info

Latency is a particular problem with lower-end PC laptops. Often the standard soundcard isn't up to the job of running audio applications. In this case, an external USB or FireWire, or special laptop PCI audio card is the solution.

Tip

If you tick the Play in Background option, you'll be able to play sound from Reason even when the program is hidden or behind another program.

Figure 1.13
Audio driver selection on the PC

A note about audio drivers

On a PC, audio hardware will have an ASIO driver supplied with it. Choose this driver to use with the device. Alternatively, use the DirectX or ASIO multimedia driver, but only if a specific ASIO driver isn't available.

On Mac OS 9, audio hardware will have a dedicated ASIO driver which you should select. On Mac OSX, CoreAudio should be selected to use the internal audio hardware, or the specific driver that controls your third-party device should be selected. For example if you have an M-Audio Audiophile USB, its name will appear as an option in the list for you to choose.

MIDI settings

In Reason 2.5

From the dropdown menu you can select which device to use for MIDI input. In many cases this will be the same as the audio device, as most cards offer both audio and MIDI in and out. If you have separate audio and MIDI devices, Reason will happily use them both at the same time. There are 16 standard MIDI channels but a safe bet is to use channel 1 on all your devices when setting up communication.

Advanced MIDI lets you configure Reason to receive MIDI input from external sources for the purpose of remote control or sync. Usually you will have one MIDI interface handling all communication so that is the one to choose. If you're not syncing Reason or hooking it up to any external sequencers you don't need to worry about these settings.

In Reason 3

Reason 3 does away with the MIDI tab and replaces it with one called Control Surfaces and Keyboards. This is because it has a new system of handling MIDI communication called Remote. Instead of reading from a single device, Reason 3 can now receive data from multiple MIDI controllers at the same time. The point of this is to make it much easier to play your Reason system. Instead of being predominantly a studio tool it can now be used much more easily as a live performance tool as well. Many people have a USB MIDI controller keyboard, or a standard keyboard with realtime controllers like knobs and sliders. Reason 3 has built-in support for a wide range of controllers from leading manufacturers, and allows you to customise setups for keyboards that aren't supported out of the box. Support for new models will be added as they come onto the market. As templates are stored in a folder independent of the program itself, this will not require any program updates but rather a simple drag-and-drop. Here are some things to note about the Remote system.

Figure 1.14
Reason 3 has a new way to handle incoming MIDI traffic

When you install and boot Reason 3 for the first time it will scan your system for any installed drivers relating to MIDI controller devices. If you are adding devices with drivers later, there is an auto-detect button on the Preferences > Control Surfaces dialogue box.

If Reason does pick up such a device, it will automatically map its realtime knobs and sliders to the most useful controls on whichever module in the rack you select. Typically, sliders will correspond to mixer channels or filter controls on an instrument. Knobs on a keyboard will probably be mapped to filter or pan controls. You can remap these, but for everyday purposes the default settings are useful. When you get into locking surfaces later on, you may also have a choice of using two different built-in mapping configurations, depending on your controller and the device you're trying to control.

In the list of attached surfaces you can specify by ticking or unticking the box whether each should be used with Reason. You may have a controller accessing

Figure 1.15
Auto-Detect Surfaces

Tip

If you select a controller device from the list of available models, look out for any information that is displayed next to its picture in the Control Surface setup window. Some devices have idiosyncrasies that need to be remembered when setting up, such as a particular setting that has to be made or a channel that has to be active.

another program and not want it to interfere with Reason. In this situation, uncheck the box. The Add, Edit and Delete buttons let you manage your list of controllers.

If your MIDI keyboard is not picked up, or is connected via a MIDI interface rather than USB or FireWire, you can make Reason pick it up by clicking the Add button. Select the manufacturer or choose Other if it isn't displayed. Then from the Model menu choose what kind of keyboard it is. If your MIDI interface is not automatically picked up, press the Find button and press a key on the keyboard. Using MIDI Learn, Reason will pick it up and remember it.

Figure 1.16
Use the Add menu to add further controllers to use with Reason

The more realtime controllers you have on your keyboard, the better your control over Reason will be. A small keyboard will offer basic controls, but a bigger one like the M-Audio Keystation Pro 88 or a dedicated control surface like a Mackie Control will give you much more comprehensive options if you happen to own one. Reason 3 even supports motorized faders and device naming on dedicated control surfaces.

The way to manage the multiple devices is to lock them to devices in the rack. The controller specified as the Master Keyboard in the preferences will always follow the MIDI input (i.e. play whichever module you select in the rack). However, any number of subsequent controllers can be added. By selecting Options > Surface Locking you can select any available controller and lock it to any available module. This means it will always just control that module, at least until you unlock them from each other. The Master Keyboard can't be locked, unless you specify that Reason should not use a Master keyboard.

Figure 1.17
Locking devices to modules in the rack allows more hands-on control by several people

In use

By having more than one control surface connected at once you can greatly extend the usefulness of Reason. Here are a couple of examples.

The most obvious application for the Remote system is to have several people controlling the same Reason system off the same computer at the same time. With several USB keyboards connected, or several MIDI keyboards via an interface, or a mixture of the two systems, you can share the same project. By locking each device to a module you can all have independent control over tweaking your own instruments in realtime. This is particularly interesting if you are using Combinator patches with sequencers inside them. As Reason outputs usually to a single stereo out, the sum total of your performance can be put through a single stereo amp channel.

Figure 1.18
A USB MIDI controller locked to the mixer is a great way of 'playing' your system

Another interesting application would be to have a controller locked to the mixer, and a keyboard then playing whatever you point it at. In this way you can have control over the mix of a project including solo and mute, pan, levels and effects settings as it is playing and as you are playing along with it.

You can mix and match these ideas to have, say, control over the mixer and several instruments yourself, but with further people controlling other instruments from the same project.

If you discover that the auto-mapping isn't quite to your taste, or you have a more generic MIDI controller keyboard, you can re-map controls easily. By selecting Options > Remote Override Edit Mode you can choose a module in the rack to map. The modules are greyed out, and coloured symbols denote the parameters that can be mapped. If you double-click on a parameter it displays a lightning bolt. When you move a controller on your keyboard, or press a note, Reason maps that note or switch to the parameter you have selected.

If you control + click or right-click on a parameter in this mode, a separate window appears to let you choose specifically which controller device should be used, and which type of control message should be read. By clicking the Learn button here you can see precisely what type of control you are pressing or turning on your

Figure 1.19
Re-mapping realtime controllers to controls on Reason's modules

Tip

Leave the mouse pointer over a control for two seconds to display a tooltip telling you the map status of that parameter.

Info

If you try to map the same key to two separate parameters, Reason will warn you of the fact and you will have to choose one or the other.

Figure 1.20
Keyboard Control Mode

Info

In Remote Override Edit Mode, mapped parameters display as orange or yellow lightning bolts. Every other symbol represents an un-mapped parameter.

Tip

If you set up specific maps, say for a generic MIDI keyboard, they are saved with the song file. In order to be able to easily use them again and again it's a good idea to save them once as a template file, then open and save this under a new file name each time you start a project. Otherwise you may have to re-specify this custom mapping each time.

keyboard. Once a control has been mapped, this window will also let you edit that mapping.

Even keys on the keyboard can be used as triggers, although they work as on/off switches rather than variables. Mapping a key to a knob or slider and then pressing it will change values between zero and 100 per cent. So you could for example have part of a keyboard or even a dedicated keyboard with controls mapped simply to muting and enabling channels, switching effects on and off or bypassing devices entirely.

There is an additional menu of extra, system-specific overrides that you can map independently by selecting Options > Additional Remote Overrides. These include undo / redo, auto-quantize, patch selection and so on. With a bit of planning and some sticky labels on your keys to remind you what they trigger, you can control almost every aspect of a Reason song in a live setting without ever touching the mouse.

Sound locations

Reason 2.5

When you open a patch or file browser in Reason there are some special shortcut buttons available. The four folder buttons correspond to sound locations set in the preferences. It's good practice to keep your ReFills and samples properly organized in a few folders, or even just in one. In the Sound Locations preference page, you can set up to four locations that Reason will remember and the buttons in the file browser will jump you straight to those folders. This can save you a huge amount of time in wandering around your hard drive looking for files.

A good way to organize sounds might be to have one folder for ReFills, one for samples and one for your own patches. Hit the cross next to the location buttons to delete the links and specify a new one.

Reason 3

In Reason 3 the Sound Locations section is removed. This function is now incorporated into the new browser. See the next chapter for detailed information on this.

Working methods

Inside the Reason folder are a number of PDF files, including the Operation Manual and some notes about the effect devices. Although it may seem a bit tedious to go through it, it's worth at least one read through to familiarise yourself with some of the terminology and concepts used in the program. The manual is very well written and fairly exhaustive. If you're using Acrobat or Preview (Mac OSX only) to read the PDF, as you probably will be, don't forget the search functions. Typing a word or a sentence into the search box will show all instances of the words in the document. This is sometimes better than relying on chapter headings to find information.

Figure 2.1
Always read the manual at least once!

The Concept

It's fairly clear that Reason is based on the idea of a rack of instruments and effects. This makes it easier to get the hang of, and as an added bonus it looks pretty cool as well. It's designed to look familiar while retaining the advantages of using software – for example the ability to save and load, to duplicate, copy and paste and

Figure 2.2

The rack, sequencer and transport

to have as many modules as your hardware can run. Think of it as halfway between software and hardware. Faders, buttons and switches all move like they do in real life. On the other hand, menus and file browsers offer the kind of speedy workflow that you can't get with real instruments.

The Windows

Real hardware, of course, has things on the back of it like ports and master controls. Pressing the Tab key rotates the rack 180 degrees so that you can use them. Reason's window can be extended upwards and downwards, but not left or right. Pressing the small button at the extreme top right of the window will detach the sequencer from the rack. This can also be done by selecting Windows > Detach Sequencer Window. This is particularly useful for navigating projects as it means you can have more of the timeline on the screen. There's no need for the rack to extend outwards, as the modules are all a set width. The sequencer, however, can be zoomed and scrolled. This is handy if you're in Edit mode. If you're very lucky and have two monitors, use one screen for the rack and one for the sequencer.

The line that divides the rack and the sequencer can be dragged up or down to alter the proportion of space taken up by each side. To maximise the sequencer, click the small button at the top right of its section. To maximise the rack, click the similar button at its top right corner. Click either again to return to a split screen. Being able to maximise the sequencer in Edit mode is great when you have to view multiple controller lanes and data at the same time.

Info

Reason's rack is, in theory, endless. It will literally house as many instruments and effects as your computer can cope with. As your mixer runs out of channels, create a second mixer and chain it to the first.

Tip

Press the Tab key to spin the rack around, and again to spin it back.

Tip

Choose Options > Show Cables to show and hide the patch cables linking the modules.

Figure 2.3
Detach the two elements, rack and sequencer. Spread them over two screens if you can!

Things to remember

Reason is a MIDI sequencer. You can't record audio straight into it. It's self-contained and doesn't support external plugins of any kind. A Reason song file doesn't contain any audio data – consisting of MIDI, it's a series of instructions. So if you move projects between machines, your sounds won't go with you unless you make a point of copying the ReFills and samples as well.

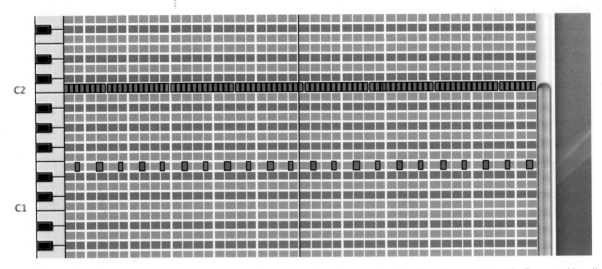

Figure 2.4
Reason works with MIDI, triggering audio samples and generating synthesized sounds

There are often a number of ways of achieving the same goal in Reason. Usually these are by dropdown menu or by contextual menu, and sometimes by keyboard shortcut. Most things in Reason are contextual, which means that you get different options depending on what you've clicked on. For example, control + clicking somewhere in the rack brings up one menu, but control + clicking on the sequencer brings up another. The part of the window that you select is outlined in light blue, which is how to tell which part you're working on. If you perform a command such as delete, and the wrong thing disappears, it's probably because you had something selected other than the item you wanted to delete. It's good practice to click on a module or a sequencer track once to make sure it's selected before you start modifying it.

Info

ReFills are special Reason Soundbanks containing all the patches and audio files you need to make music. They aren't folders and they aren't programs, and can't be opened except from within Reason, via an instrument or effect module.

Info

There are lots of free and commercial ReFills available for download or mail order. A lot of major sample CD companies now release their sounds in ReFill as well as other formats.

Tip

Multiple select modules in the rack by holding shift and clicking on them. This also allows the selecting of non-sequential items, so you could choose the first, fourth and sixth items, then hit delete to get rid of them.

Figure 2.5
Selecting non-sequential modules

The Transport panel

The Transport panel is always present, even if you split up the two sections. It contains all the tools you need to control playback and recording. It can actually be minimized so as to be almost invisible by clicking the small arrow on its far left hand side, but it takes up so little space anyway that you won't end up hiding it very often, if ever. The main Transport panel controls are the same as the controls on a tape machine. Basic operations like play, stop and record are mapped to simple key presses.

Tempo and time signature

The left tempo field is where you set the tempo from 1 to 999 beats per minute. Typically, ambient music is around 75-95 BPM, hip hop around 80-100BPM and dance music 100BPM and above. The field on the right lets you set very precise divisions of 1/1000BPM, if you need for some reason to have an odd speed. Using the plus and minus keys on the numeric keypad will increase or decrease the tempo in increments of 1BPM (Figure 2.6).

Click the time signature up / down arrows to control the master time signature. 4/4 is by far the most commonly used timebase, but you are by no means limited to it. Tracks with unusual time signatures often sound more interesting. The grid and the click will change to follow the new values if you alter them.

Locators

The left and right locators are incredibly useful. A lot of the time it's necessary to loop sections while you build up layers of music. The locators tell Reason where to start and end loops, as well as how much to export when you've finished. There are four ways to set locator positions.

- Pick up and drag the locators on the timeline
- Double click the number fields in the transport panel and enter a numerical value for where you want it to go. The fields are divided by bar and beat. So entering 12.2.1 would put the locator at the second beat of bar 12.
- Click and hold the mouse on a number field and drag the pointer up or down, or left and right. Doing this on the left field scrolls quickest, on the middle field it's slower and on the right field slowest but most precise.
- Alt + click on the bar display in the timeline to set the left locator. Option + click to set the right locator. Shift + click in the same area to set the end marker for the whole project. The end marker can be dragged further to the right to extend the overall length of a project.

The same principles apply to the song position controls under the play and record buttons. Jump to a position in a song by clicking, holding and dragging rather than scrolling around the timeline.

Info

Reason doesn't allow tempo changes within a track

Figure 2.6
Setting the Tempo

Figure 2.7
The left and right locators are crucial to working in Reason

Figure 2.7
The left and right locators are crucial to working in Reason

Other Transport tricks

Thc Click track, which will be crucial to recording in time, is switched on and off, and its level set, from the Transport Panel (Figure 2.8).

If you have automated a parameter, but then start to change it when it is in automated mode, the Automation Punched In light comes on to show that you are overriding some automation. This is only temporary for as long as the track is playing.

If sounds are starting to distort, check the Audio Out Clipping indicator on the Transport Panel. If it has lit up, the hardware interface is being fed levels that are too high. Try reducing the level of individual mixer channels or the master fader level. Level meters should be in the yellow and orange but not the red (Figure 2.9).

Figure 2.8 (left)
The all-important click control

Figure 2.9 (right)
The Audio Clipping Indicator

CPU level indicator is not an absolute measure of CPU use. For example if it read 100%, it would not mean that Reason was using the computer's whole capacity. It displays how much power Reason's audio engine is using. Audio processing gets priority over graphics and MIDI, which have to share what's left over. If this meter is pushing into the red, it's time to simplify your song or buy a faster computer.

The Hardware Interface

This is where you manage how Reason communicates with the rest of your system. Divided into two sections, the Hardware Interface can't be deleted, and so is always present in the rack. Reason always has to be able to transmit sound and realistically will always have to receive MIDI, so you'll always need the hardware interface. It is split into two sections.

Tip

The MIDI sync controls are only to be activated if you want to control Reason from an external device. Pressing this button will disable the transport controls.

Figure 2.10
The Hardware
Interface

MIDI In Device

- Reason can accept up to 64 channels of MIDI input. This is split into 4 busses, each with 16 MIDI channels.
- The most common way of routing MIDI is via the Sequencer. When you select a track, the device connected to that track will automatically receive MIDI input. A green level meter on the sequencer track will light to show MIDI received.
- Using this method, you only need set the master MIDI channel once in the preferences, and MIDI in will go to whichever instrument you select.
- If you have a more advanced MIDI interface, you can use the preferences to set up to four MIDI input busses, each with 16 channels. This is the mode to use if you want to control Reason's instruments from an external sequencer, or send information on several MIDI channels at once.
- In this mode, you have to use the dropdown menu by each MIDI in channel to specify which instrument to route signal to. A list of all available instrument modules will appear in the dropdown list.
- A red LED blinking by each MIDI channel indicates MIDI received on that channel. If it isn't coming through correctly, check that your keyboard or sequencer is transmitting on the correct channel and that Reason's preferences are set correctly to receive.
- You can use the bus select buttons at the top of the interface to choose which of the four busses is on view.
- With the new Remote system, multiple MIDI in devices can be used at the same time.

Figure 2.11
The MIDI interface lets you manage multiple MIDI inputs

Audio Out Device

- Reason allows for up to 64 channels of audio output, if your hardware has that many. In reality you probably won't use more than 8 or 10 channels unless you're using ReWire.
- You activate the outputs in the Preferences > Audio window. Use the Active Channels button.
- One use for multiple outputs is if you are routing sound out of Reason to an external mixing desk or through outboard effects. By setting up tracks to fire straight out of your soundcard's outputs, say, drum tracks to a compressor and pads to a reverb unit, you could process them externally.
- If you do this, it's best to do the whole track through an external mixer, as getting the processed sound back into Reason in realtime would be tricky.
- You can still use Reason's effects and mixer before sending sound through hardware outputs, creating a signal chain. This is due to its modular nature, and the fact that you can pick up and re-patch cables as you like. Just follow the chain through to make sure the sound is being sent to and from the right place.
- The most likely use for the 64 outputs is with ReWire, where audio is streamed from Reason into the mixer of another sequencer such as Cubase, Logic or Sonar.

Figure 2.12
From the Audio Out panel you can route any
audio signal to your soundcard, or to ReWire

The Browser

Reason 3 sports a very greatly improved browser, which had remained much the same in all previous versions of Reason. Now it's almost like a program within a program. Made up of different regions, it has a number of new search and preview functions.

The Sound Locations tab from previous Reason versions has been moved to the Browser. By navigating to a folder on your hard drive and drag + dropping it into the Locations window you can build up a list of folder shortcuts with no limit on the number of folders. To remove items from this list, control+click or right-click and select Remove.

Figure 2.13
The New Browser, much extended

To save time when locating your favourite patches, use the Favourites window. Create a new list, right-click or control+click to rename it and then drag any number of your favourite patches to the list for instant location. This is useful when playing live or for inspiration when composing on-the-fly.

The search section at the top is very powerful and lets you be very specific about the files you find. The first level of filtering is by location type. These go from the narrow (search current folder) to medium (search within User Locations) to the broad (search all local disks). The two arrows will take you back or forward through all the locations you have previously searched during that session.

To jump to a hierarchical view of the computer's disks, choose Desktop from the Locations list. Then, the dropdown menu will allow access to all levels of the drives. To save time, drop local hard drives into the Locations window so that they are accessible with a single click.

Reason's browser can navigate to any volume, be it an internal or FireWire hard drive, CD / DVD, USB flash drive, networked volume or even iPod. It can load sounds from any of these. However, if any of these are disconnected later, Reason won't be able to find the sounds. Remember a Reason project file only contains links to sounds, not the sounds themselves. Working from CD or networked volume will also slow you down considerably. A much better idea is to keep everything on internal hard drives.

Info

You can only drag patches, samples or REX files to a Favourites list. You can't drag ReFills or folders.

Figure 2.14
Set up and name favourites lists containing patches and samples

Figure 2.15
Advanced searching

One of the greatest new features in Reason 3 is that the Browser now actually loads patches as you select them, meaning you can play and hear them from within the Browser itself! Before, you had to actually load the whole patch to hear what it sounded like, which could result in a lot of time spent going through patches, deciding they weren't appropriate and then browsing and loading again until you found one. That's now a thing of the past. As patches are selected they are loaded automatically. Samples and REX files are previewed as you select them. You can switch Autoplay on or off and manually stop or start samples and set volume using the Audition window. The volume slider controls the levels of audio files that audition, not MIDI-triggered instruments.

Figure 2.16
You can preview sounds in the Browser in Reason 3

The same applies to effects. You can't 'play' an effect but you can play through it. So if you have a guitar sound loaded into an NN-XT, for example, then attach an effect unit to it, you can use the browser to audition different effect patches for that module. As you move between them, keep playing the keyboard and you'll hear the guitar sound effected in different ways. This is the case with every effect module.

The Search For text box lets you perform a text search for patches and files. This is very useful because it will find all files containing the word(s) you enter, regardless of file type. For example, if you search for 'Bass' you will be presented with every file containing the word Bass. You can limit this by using the Show menu to specify whether to view all instruments, all effects or Combinator patches. If you're browsing for an effect patch you won't want to see all the instrument patches, just the effects. Furthermore, the results can be sorted by clicking the column names. For example, to sort them by style click the Parent column. For an alphabetical list, click the Name column and so on. The Browser also displays helpful information in the Details section about each patch you select, although this tends to be more relevant for Combinator patches.

Name	Parent	Modified	Size
Pusher Upright Bass.cmb	Acoustic Bass	02/0... 15:56	4 kB
Upright Bass.sxt	Acoustic Bass	02/0... 15:56	29 kB
Upright II.sxt	Acoustic Bass	02/0... 15:56	18 kB
Upright Old...htclub.cmb	Acoustic Bass	02/0... 15:56	3 kB
Upright Old...htclub.cmb	Acoustic Bass	02/0... 15:56	3 kB
Upright+Harm.sxt	Acoustic Bass	02/0... 15:56	38 kB
UprightHarmonics.sxt	Acoustic Bass	02/0... 15:56	9 kB
Ac TightNBassy.sxt	Acoustic Guitar	02/0... 15:56	21 kB
2StepBass.xwv	Bass	02/0... 15:56	1 kB
4am Bass.zyp	Bass	02/0... 15:56	1 kB
80s Syn bass.xwv	Bass	02/0... 15:56	1 kB
AcBss MW Mute.zyp	Bass	02/0... 15:56	1 kB

Figure 2.17
Sorting search results by column

When you browse from a certain type of device, the Show menu will alter to reflect that. If you browse from a Subtractor for instance, it will default to showing only Subtractor patches because this is probably what you're after. However you can always switch this menu to show all instruments, displaying all patches for all modules.

You don't have to enter any text to search. For example, if you browse from an RV-7000 effect module and then select Search in User Locations and Show RV7000 patches but don't enter anything into the text field, you will get a list of every patch within your Location folders that can be loaded by this module. The same applies to any other module.

Searching Local Disks, or having an entire drive (like Macintosh HD or the C: drive) in the Locations list can considerably slow down a search for files, as Reason has to sort through thousands of files. It's a much better idea to keep patches and sounds in individual folders and put these in the Favourites list, so Reason isn't having to scour pointless system and library folders. In this case you must also of course use the Search In User Locations or Current Folder options.

You can create devices directly from the Browser, regardless of the type of module you browsed from. For example, let's say you browse in from a Subtractor. You search for 'Lead' and find a great Lead synth patch, but it's for a Mâlstrom. Where previously you would have had to go back a load a Mâlstrom, then re-browse, now you can just load one by pressing OK in the browser. In fact, as you audition different patches you can see that Reason loads the relevant module in the rack, replacing the module you browsed from.

When you run a search for a particular word and view the results in a list, you can use the folder dropdown menu (next to the two arrows) to jump to the parent folder of that patch. This is because such a search can turn up varied results. Jumping to the parent folder of a patch will show you what category it is in as well as giving you quick access to other patches in that category (Figure 2.18).

Figure 2.18
Jump to the parent folder of a patch to see patches of similar type

There is a new item in the Create menu called Create Device by Browsing Patches. essentially, if you start from anywhere in the rack (even an empty rack), you can browse for any kind of patch, audition it and Reason will load it in the background. This is great for creativity and spontenaiety as it means you don't have to create a device and then decide on a sound, you can browse a whole palette of sounds and be inspired (Figure 2.19).

Figure 2.19
Create devices by browsing patches, rather than having to create then load

If you browse from the sample section (not patch section) of an NN-19 and find a REX file, you can expand that REX file within the browser to see its constituent parts, and then load a single slice into the NN-19. The same applies if you browse from the sample button (not patch button) on any channel in a ReDrum.

Figure 2.20
Browse from the sample load button of a sampler and you can view and load the individual slices of REX files

Creating devices

R eason projects are constructed by creating devices in the rack, then playing MIDI into the sequencer, which has tracks connected to those devices. Before you can hear any sounds you have to create some modules. A few points to remember about devices:

- Reason has a set number of devices and doesn't support third-party plugins of any kind. However, because modules can be freely patched together, it is still a very flexible program.
- The Audio and MIDI interfaces at the top of the rack are always present.
- You can create as many devices as your computer can handle. Some are more power-hungry than others, so 50 ReDrums is not the same power drain as 50 Malströms. Different patches for the same instrument also use different amounts of power.
- Like a real studio setup, everything in Reason runs through a mixer. You're not limited to one mixer - several can be chained together.
- Everything can be unplugged and re-patched, and there's no limit on how many stages a source can go through before it reaches the desk. For example, a sampler could run through one, ten or fifty effect modules before it got to the desk.

Figure 3.1
The Create menu

The simplest way to create a device is to go to the Create menu at the top and select which kind of device to insert. You should always start with a mixer. Otherwise, the first instrument you create will be wired straight to the hardware interface, and subsequent instruments you create won't output any sound until connected to more audio outputs on the hardware interface. Whilst this works and is possible, it's a labour-intensive way to use Reason. It's far better to use a mixer.

Reason automatically routes the outputs of instruments into the mixer. This means that you can create a device and know that it will be plugged into the next available mixer channel for you. If you have disconnected a device (Edit > Disconnect Device) or re-patched it and want it routed straight back into the mixer, select it and choose Edit > Auto-Route Device, and Reason will re-patch it into the next available mixer channel.

Figure 3.2
Auto-routing devices if they have been
disconnected

There's no set order in which you have to create devices, although it makes sense to have the mixer at the top (Figure 3.2).

Tips for working with devices

- Deleting devices is as simple as selecting them and hitting backspace. Also you can select the device and select Edit > Delete Device.
- Press command + delete (Mac) or control + delete (PC) to get rid of a device without the confirmation box popping up.
- Hold down shift + click to select multiple and non-sequential devices in the rack.
- Each module has a small arrow at the top left corner. Click on it to expand or minimize the device. Alt + clicking it will expand or minimize every device in the rack at once. This saves a lot of time when working with many devices in a rack. It also works when the rack is spun around.
- Instrument devices can be dragged up and down and re-ordered in the rack, but only when they are picked up by their end panels, between the screws. This works whether they are minimized or maximized. They can also be re-ordered in the sequencer. Neither of these operations alters the order in which they are connected to the mixer.
- Control + click (Mac) or right click (PC) on an empty section of the rack brings up the same menu as you get from the Create option at the top (Figure 3.3).
- If you delete a device connected between two devices, Reason automatically compensates by reconnecting the two remaining devices. So for example if you have a sampler running into a reverb unit and then on into the mixer, then you delete the reverb unit, the sampler will be patched directly into the mixer.
- If you duplicate a device in the rack by dragging it or using copy and paste, it is not automatically routed. If you want it to be, hold down the Shift key as you drag / copy.

Figure 3.3
The contextual menu

- If you re-order a device by dragging it up or down the rack, it stays plugged into the same mixer channel. If you want it to move to a different mixer channel based on its new position in the rack, hold down Shift while you drag it.
- To force Reason not to auto-route a device when you create it, hold down the Shift key.
- Using the up and down arrows on the keyboard will quickly scroll up or down the rack, selecting modules as you go.

Types of devices

Reason has two main types of modules – instruments and effects. Within these there are some subdivisions. Some of the instruments are synthesizers, which generate sounds, and some are sample-based, meaning that they use existing audio samples to play back sounds. Of the effect devices, most apply an effect to an audio signal, but a couple are routing modules which send CV signal rather than audio. Sample-based modules tend to be less power hungry. Synth modules use more CPU, especially if a patch uses lots of oscillators and filters.

Cables

Patch cables show you how things are connected to each other. They are visible when you spin the rack around to view the back.

Figure 3.4
Reason's lifeblood – the patch cables

Tip

Select Options > Show Cables or press Command + L (Mac) or Control + L (PC) to toggle their visibility on and off. Useful if many cables are obscuring your view.

Tip

It can be frustrating trying to track a patch cable from source to destination. Leave the mouse pointer over a connection for a few seconds and a tooltip will appear, telling you where the cable goes.

Cables can be picked up and plugged in at either end. Audio cables and ports are larger, CV cables and ports are smaller. You can't plug an audio lead into a CV port or vice versa, as the two carry different types of signal. Cables are also colour coded for convenience.

- Audio cables are different shades of red
- CV connections are shown in shades of yellow
- Connections to and from effects modules are shown in green.

As well as clicking on a port to plug a cable into it, you can click or right-click on a port. A list of all the devices in the rack will appear. From this menu you can choose any available port on any device which will accept the connection you're trying to make. The device you're connecting from will be greyed out, as will any devices which won't accept connections from your selected module. This menu also has a Disconnect option. Disconnecting can also be done by picking up a cable and dragging it away from a jack plug.

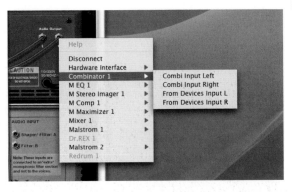

Figure 3.5
The contextual menu for a port displays all
connections in the project to which that
signal could be routed

The instrument modules have different types of outputs. The Subtractor, for example, is a monophonic instrument and so only has one output. The Dr:Rex, Malström and NN-19 have stereo audio outputs, and the ReDrum and NN-XT sampler have multiple separate audio outputs, although used in a simple way they only need a stereo pair.

Tip

As you drag a cable over ports, suitable ones will light up in red. If a port doesn't light up, you can't connect that particular cable to it.

Figure 3.6
Certain modules like the ReDrum and NN-XT
have separate audio outputs for their many
channels

ReWire

Reason doesn't record audio, but this is something that you will probably want to do when you're making music. Being able to put vocals or live instruments over your Reason tracks is fairly crucial to a lot of people. You can of course mix a track down from Reason and import it into another program to overlay more sounds, but then you lose all editability on the Reason track.

Happily, Reason incorporates a technology called ReWire which allows it to be synchronized with other sequencers. It has a number of features:

- ReWire allows the streaming of separate audio channels between audio applications. For example, between Reason and Cubase. Up to 256 are supported.

Figure 3.7
Reason ReWired to Cubase SX

- Both programs synchronize together perfectly, and the transport controls from one will control the other. So pressing play in Cubase will also play Reason. Moving the playhead in Reason will move it to the same position in Cubase and so on.
- Both programs can share the same sound card, which can otherwise often be problematic when using two applications with ASIO drivers.
- ReWire is mostly automatic and doesn't require any setting up

Info

Reason is the ReWire Slave. The other sequencer, like Logic, Cubase or Sonar, is the ReWire Master. Reason always slaves to a Master when in ReWire mode (Figure 3.8).

All ReWire connections from Reason are done through the hardware interface at the top of the rack. It's a lot like what happens if you route audio straight out to the outputs of a soundcard, only in this case rather than a soundcard, the signal is sent to the mixer of your Master program, such as Cubase. Master programs generally automatically detect the presence of Reason and add it to their options menus without you having to do anything. Any ReWire Master program will have a section to enable ReWire inputs. In Cubase this is under the Devices menu. A window opens that lets you activate and rename ReWire channels which correspond directly to the ports on Reason's hardware interface. Mix L and Mix R are the main stereo outputs from Reason's mixer. This is the simplest way to use ReWire, and means that the whole mix is streamed through on a stereo channel. A mixer in Reason will automatically be routed to channels 1 and 2 on the Hardware Interface, but there's nothing to stop you moving them to any other ports.

Tip

If you are using Reason ReWired to another sequencer, always boot the main sequencer first and Reason second. Otherwise ReWire won't work. Also when finished, quit Reason first.

Tip

Booting Reason first and another sequencer second means both will operate as separate programs. This may cause problems if they try to access the same soundcard.

Info

In Mac OS9, running Reason in ReWire mode means you should increase the memory allocation to the host sequencer, as it will become more resource-hungry. This only applies to versions of Reason earlier than 3.

Figure 3.9
Some instruments being sent directly out to ReWire from Reason...

Figure 3.10
...and received in Cubase SX

Info

Left and Right locators and the loop on/off control, when set in one program will be reflected in the other.

Things to remember when using ReWire

The host application always sets the master tempo. Altering the tempo in Reason will affect both programs, unless you are using automated tempo changes (a tempo track) in the host program. In this case, changing the tempo in Reason has no effect.

Routing a stereo mix through from Reason is good, but means you can't process any Reason tracks individually in your host's mixer. It's better to start separating instruments off and assigning them to their own ReWire channels. This gives you much more flexibility.

You can assign MIDI tracks in your host sequencer to play Reason's instruments, without needing to have Reason in the foreground. The names of the instruments will appear in the list of available MIDI destinations on the MIDI track. You can set MIDI to be routed through from the host to Reason to play the track live, and also to assign existing MIDI tracks in the host to use Reason's instruments rather than their own virtual synths.

Figure 3.11
Reason's instruments are playable via MIDI tracks in the host sequencer

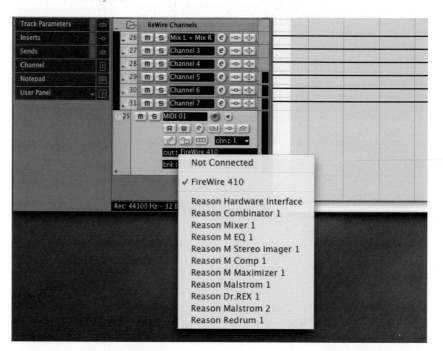

When you name instruments in Reason, either on the module or in the sequencer, that name is the one that is broadcast over ReWire. It's good practice to name things properly, or you end up with a list of ReDrum 1, ReDrum 2 and so on.

Converting ReWire to audio

Audio streamed into a host from Reason over ReWire is treated like any other audio channel. That is, you can apply effects and EQ to it. This means that you can use VST, Audio Unit, RTAS or DXi effects on Reason's instruments, which sort of gets around its not supporting external plugins. So in practice you may well be able to leave channels as ReWire, as they will be exported with any final mixdown from your host just as if they existed as audio within the host.

Figure 3.12
ReWire channels are included in audio mixdowns from the host sequencer

In some situations you may want to convert ReWire outputs to audio files. For example, to perform edits or special effects that are easier to achieve on an audio file than a MIDI file. You may also want to finish a project entirely in your host sequencer and not have to boot Reason up if the final arrangement is correct for the MIDI parts. The easiest way to turn ReWire into audio is to solo the relevant ReWire tracks in the host sequencer and bounce them down. In Cubase, the process would go something like this.

- Solo one or more ReWire tracks in the Cubase mixer. Choose only the ones you want to convert.
- Set the L and R locators over the section you need. Refer to Reason's sequencer here, as there will be no audio material in Cubase yet to show where to begin and end. Turn looping off.
- Select File > Audio Mixdown (or the equivalent in your sequencer).
- If there is an option, choose to import the newly created file onto a new audio track in the host sequencer. In Cubase this is Import to Audio track and Import to Pool. As the file is exported, any automation, EQ and effects applied in Cubase are included in the rendered file.
- The file is imported, so disable the ReWire channel you just rendered down, or the original will continue to play through from Reason.

If there is no auto-import option in your host's export dialogue box, make sure you know where the file is being saved to then use File > Import in the host to bring the rendered file back into the host project. It is also possible of course to export loops or tracks from Reason to your hard drive, then import them to the host in this way, without using ReWire. The disadvantage of this is that you have to be happy with the Reason tracks before you export them, as the notes will stop being editable.

Tip

Having ReWire channels activated uses processing power, so only activate as many as you're using. You can switch them on or off at any point.

Figure 3.13
You may have to render tracks out through the host sequencer, then bring them back in as audio files onto new tracks

The Mixer

R eason's mixer works in the same way as a real hardware mixer. If you have experience with real mixers it will make a lot of sense. If you don't, it's a good way to learn about how routing and mixing work. In all probability, everything you do in Reason will involve using at least one mixer.

A mixer has 14 channel strips, each with separate level, EQ, Pan, solo / mute and aux controls. Each channel is stereo, though to save space only a single LED meter is shown per channel. There's also a master fader and an effect return section. Each channel strip has a signal path, but it doesn't correspond to the physical order of the knobs on the channel.

Tip

A s you create devices in the rack, they are automatically placed on the next available mixer channel. If you delete a device from the middle of the rack then create a new one, Reason will use the mixer channel that was just vacated, so you don't have to shuffle channels around.

Figure 4.1
Reason's mixer

Aux returns

The aux return section at the top right of the mixer is where you control the levels of the send effects that you attach to the mixer. When the mixer is selected (with a light blue outline around it) and you select Create and then an effect module, the effect is attached to the mixer as a send effect, and automatically routed to the next available aux channel. If you spin the rack around you will see Reason automatically patches send effects to the aux return section (Figure 4.2).

Figure 4.2
Effects created when the mixer is selected
are automatically routed as sends

Send effects

In Reason, as in other sequencers and real hardware studios, effects can be applied in two main ways. As inserts or sends. Insert effects are attached between an instrument and the mixer, so the mixer receives signal that has already been effected. Send effects are attached to the mixer, and then become available to every channel on the mixer. In many situations you will want to have a few standard effects that are applied to every channel. Typically this might be a reverb, a compressor and a delay unit. Most of the tracks in your project may need a small amount of reverb on them. Applying a reverb unit to every instrument as an insert is both time consuming and power-hungry. Instead, add a reverb as a send effect and then by increasing the aux send for the channel that reverb is attached to, you apply reverb to the channel. Every channel in a mixer can share each of the four send effects. The trick is to make one setting on the unit itself, then use the aux send levels on the channels to set how much effect is applied to each channel. So for example, if channel 1 had its aux1 send set at 127 but channel 2 had it set to 10, both channels would be going through the same send effect, but channel 1 would have much more effect applied. By altering the aux return level on the mixer you can place a limit on the maximum effect level that will be applied. When you create a send effect its return level defaults to 100, which is probably adequate for most uses. To get bigger effects you can raise this level to 127.

Tip

Send effects can't be renamed on the mixer but if you rename the effect module itself, the name will change on the mixer as well.

Tip

To quickly reset any knob in Reason to its default value or zero, click on it whilst holding command (Mac) or Control (PC).

Figure 4.3
Using effects as sends to conserve CPU. Vary the send amounts for each channel on the mixer

Many of the controls on the mixer are knobs. The best way to move them is to click and hold on them with the mouse, then drag straight up or down. The faster you drag, the more quickly the control will move. To get better control you can go into Reason's preferences and set General > Mouse Knob Range to Very Precise. Alternatively for less specific control, set it to Normal. If you hold down the shift key as you drag the knobs, they move in much smaller increments, which can be useful, especially when automating them.

Figure 4.4
Setting the mouse knob sensitivity

Info

By using effects as sends you reduce the CPU requirements of a project. Ten channels going through one reverb send effect use a lot less power than ten reverbs applied as inserts.

The Master Fader

The master fader controls the master output of all channels in the mixer. Every channel is sent to it and then a single mixed signal is sent on, usually to the Hardware Interface. It's important to keep an eye on the master fader when mixing, as sometimes when you think the track doesn't seem loud enough, it's because the master fader is set too low. The master fader is where you can control master fade ins and fade outs for your tracks. See chapter 6 for more on this.

Why are my tracks so quiet?

A common mistake is to boost all the channels up to maximum to try to make them louder. Channels shouldn't be competing with each other – the concept of mixing is to achieve a balance of sounds. The master fader defaults to a volume level of 100, and this is a good level to work with. You can push it higher, as long as the level meters don't stay at the very top. You can go lower, but if you go too low you'll need to boost your monitoring system just to hear the track, and you'll probably also start getting hiss in the sound. If your tracks seem too quiet there are some things to check.

Figure 4.5
The master fader – small but important

- Look if the master fader is set to between 90 and 110. These are good levels to work with in general. Your guide should be the coloured LED meters. They should be well into the orange during louder sections of music, but not consistently hitting the top.
- The Audio Out Clipping indicator at the bottom left of the transport panel will light up if your overall signal is too high. Lower the master fader to correct this.
- You shouldn't really be running audio channels with the faders jammed right to the top. If the faders are nearly at full stretch and it's still not loud enough, go to the instrument itself and raise the Master Level control on it. Every instrument has a master volume control and not all default to full volume.

Figure 4.6
Keep an eye on the master level

- If an effect is applied as an insert, check that its master volume level is turned up far enough, and that the effect you're applying isn't limiting the volume of the sound passing through it. Some effects like EQ and reverb used heavily can have the unintentional effect of quietening the signal.
- If you are running in ReWire mode, be sure to check that the channels running through to the other sequencer are turned up, and that effects applied in that sequencer aren't limiting the volume.
- Remember your external hardware. If you are running instruments directly out to a real mixer, check the channel and master faders on that mixer.
- Make sure your speakers are turned up. This sounds simplistic, but it's very easy to be baffled by a quiet signal when everything looks OK, only to realise your speakers are set to low volume. Also look at your soundcard's control panel to ensure the outputs you're using are switched up properly.

Tips for mixing music

There are some good general rules for mixing regardless of platform or software. The process of mixing a track always involves some common elements such as setting levels, setting EQ and adding effects and fades. Mixing is fairly subjective, although a 'bad' mix will probably sound bad to everyone who hears it. A good mix means people probably won't notice the work that's gone into getting it right, because by definition it should just sound 'right'. A great mix will probably only be fully appreciated by music types, although it should still be your aim! Here are some things you should remember when mixing tracks.

- Take a mixdown of your track as a WAV or AIFF file, burn it to CD and listen to it on a number of different music systems. It might sound good on your expensive monitors, but not on your friend's hi-fi. Try playing it through a range of systems from high-end equipment to car stereos and personal CD players. By doing this, any problems with the mix will become evident. For example, the bass might sound right on your monitors, but be nonexistent on a smaller system. Changing the mix and trying again will help to fix this.
- Work with a decent soundcard and a decent monitoring system. A pair of old hi-fi speakers is OK but won't help you get the best possible mix.
- Don't decide on a final mix when you've been listening to the same track all day. Your ears get tired and it becomes hard to judge what sounds right and wrong. Take an hour or two off, or better still, leave it a day or two and come back with a fresh perspective.

Figure 4.8
Burn a CD of your mix and try it on other systems

- Get a second opinion. If you're working on your own, ask someone whose opinion you value to listen to the mix. Having not heard it a thousand times, they may well have some useful suggestions that you wouldn't otherwise have thought of.
- Don't mix at loud volumes. By all means turn it up a couple of times to see how the mix holds up, but constant loud monitoring won't give a true picture of how the track sounds.
- If you're doing an album, make sure all the tracks sound like they belong on the same record. That is, they are all mixed to about the same level.

Chaining mixers

Reason's modular structure means that everything can be freely patched. One result of this is that you aren't limited to having one mixer in a project. After all, if you could only have 14 channels you would run out of options fairly quickly. If you fill up your first mixer, create another one. Regardless of where it sits in the rack, Reason will know it's a mixer and connect it to the chaining inputs on the first mixer. Any instruments you create after this should be routed to the second mixer, and the mixer's master outputs will be sent back to the first mixer. It doesn't need a channel to be available on the first mixer, as chaining is handled through a special set of connections. When you've filled up the first mixer, make sure that you select the second mixer when creating further instruments, otherwise the new instru-

Figure 4.9
Chained mixers seen from the front…

Figure 4.10
…and from the back

ments won't be auto-routed. Alternatively, make sure that you have a module below the second mixer in the rack selected when creating new instruments. That way, Reason knows to connect them to the second mixer. Of course you can spin the rack around and patch the instruments yourself if you like. When mixers are chained their aux sends are connected to the chaining aux inputs on the first mixer. This means that all channels in the second mixer can access the send effects connected to the first mixer. If you only need a few more channels you can use a Line mixer instead.

Remember that although a lot of patching happens automatically, you can change it if you like. For example, you can disconnect the aux sends from the second mixer and then attach up to four effects to that mixer, using them as independent sends, available only to the channels on that mixer. Although subsequent mixers are connected automatically to the previous mixer via the chaining bus, you can of course disconnect them and route them through to separate channels on the Hardware Interface. You can create as many mixers as your system will run, so in theory you can have, say, ten mixers all connected to channels on the Hardware Interface and all outputting to separate ports on your soundcard. One application for this might be if you were making tracks with a lot of instruments, you could have a mixer for each group of sounds. One for the drums, one for the basses, the synths and so on. The other great thing about chaining mixers is that it gets around the problem of only having four send effect slots.

Figure 4.11

A complex example of routing multiple mixers straight to the Hardware Interface

Figure 4.12
Names set on the instrument will also update on the mixer

The Channel Strip

Each channel strip has some common elements. Here are some tips for using and being creative with mixer channels.

The channel names are read-only, but if you edit the name of an instrument or module, it is updated on the mixer channel that module is connected to. Get into the habit of naming modules as you create them. Otherwise you tend to end up with Dr:Rex 1, Dr:Rex 2 and so on, which is tiresome when you have to mute or solo channels and you don't know what's playing through what. Even just naming the modules after the instrument you load into them will make your life easier.

When you solo a channel, all other channels will be muted. You can solo other channels to bring them back into the mix. When you mute a channel, that channel alone is muted. Further channels can be independently muted to knock them out of the mix. If you have multiple mixers, solo and mute only affect the mixer you click on, so any channels on other mixers will need to be soloed or muted separately. In Reason 3, the sequencer also has proper solo and mute controls.

Figure 4.13
Solo and mute individual channels

Figure 4.14
Use the EQ controls to help sounds sit better in the mix

Using the pan control will help you to achieve more interesting mixes. Most records use panning to create stereo effects. For example, if you duplicate a device in the rack, connect it to the next mixer channel and duplicate its sequencer track, then pan one channel hard left and one hard right, you'll get a fuller sound from the instrument. Two instances of it will be playing at once using exactly the same notes. Label the first instrument something like Piano L and the second Piano R.

Blending sounds into a mix is often best achieved by using EQ. By pressing the EQ button to activate it for a channel, you can raise or lower the treble and bass of that channel until it sits better in the mix. Reason 2.5 has two EQ modes. Look on the back of the mixer and a switch lets you toggle between Compatible and Improved EQ modes. If you are opening songs created in an old version of Reason you can use Compatible mode to make sure they play back identically to the old version. Generally though you'll want to leave this on the Improved setting.

The Aux send controls let you vary the amount of signal that is sent to the send effects. If you press the P button, pre-fader mode is activated for aux send 4. This means that the send effects is applied after the EQ and pan controls but before the signal reaches the fader. This allows you to lower the fader completely and just hear the wet signal as passed through send effect 4.

All the controls on a mixer can be automated. If you hold down the alt key when

Figure 4.15
Automating mixer controls

clicking on a mixer control, the sequencer window will jump to edit view and display the automation timeline for that control. As a lot of automation is fine tuned using pen tools in edit mode, this is a quick way of tweaking automation without having to click through several menus. See chapter 6 for tips on automation in Reason.

The Line Mixer

Reason 3 has a mini-mixer called the 6:2 Line mixer. Its six stereo input channels are combined to a single master stereo out, which is then sent on to the main mixer or to a Combinator or other device. It has several uses. Here are some suggestions.

The Line Mixer is ideal for sub-mixing devices, especially within a Combinator patch. All the devices in a Combinator must have their outputs collected together to form a stereo output to be sent onwards to the mixer. If you create a Combinator and add devices to it one by one, only the first instrument will be auto-routed. If you create a Line mixer and then add the instruments, they will be properly routed and when you play a note, all instruments will be triggered.

Figure 4.16
The Line mixer is ideal for submixing devices within a combi

Info

Each of the six channels has level, mute, solo, pan and an aux send, so you can fine-tune the mixture of sounds within a Combi before it ever reaches the main mixer.

Tip

If you use the Line Mixer in a Combi or on its own in the rack, it can be used just to create supplementary send effects to add to the four allowed by the ReMix.

This mixer is best to use when you need to mix a few devices together, and when a full ReMix would be overkill. You can of course have any number of Line Mixers within a Combi or within the rack itself. You can manually patch any modules through a Line Mixer – it doesn't have to happen within a Combinator.

You can attach a send effect to a Line mixer and it can be controlled using the aux send and return controls. Each of the six channels can have independent amounts of the send applied. If you create a send chain, by adding a few send effects one after the other, the effects are applied together. In this way you can build up huge effects within a Combi.

Figure 4.17
A send effect connected to a Line mixer

The Sequencer

V irtual instruments are nothing without a sequencer to tell them what to play. MIDI notes are played into the sequencer, and the sequencer tracks are connected to instruments, which then output sound. As well as simple notes, the sequencer in Reason is where you control all automation and pattern data. Sequencing implies building up a track from different parts, and as well as editing notes, the sequencer is where you assemble groups of notes into whole tracks. There are two main modes in Reason – Arrange and Edit. Arrange is where you build the track and see it graphically as layers of notes. Edit is where you view and change all the parameters of an instrument or a pattern.

Figure 5.1
Toggle between Arrange and Edit modes

Sequencer basics

Every instrument in the rack must have a sequencer track associated with it if it is to play notes back. The instrument that you play from the MIDI keyboard is the one with the small MIDI plug icon next to it in the sequencer window in Reason 2.5. In Reason 3, the MIDI plug is replaced by a keyboard icon. This icon and a green level meter next to it mean that MIDI is being routed to that instrument. Click in this area on another sequencer track to send MIDI to it.

In Reason 3, multiple MIDI devices can be used at the same time. It's a good idea to have one Master keyboard which directs MIDI to whichever module you select, and have subsequent controllers locked to specific devices in the rack.

Figure 5.2
Specify a master keyboard, which will always be playable, in the preferences

Figure 5.3
Manually redirect MIDI for a sequencer track
to a different instrument

Figure 5.3
Manually redirect MIDI for a sequencer track
to a different instrument

The sequencer timeline is divided up into bars and beats. Zooming in lets you see the subdivisions of beats. Changing the time signature will change the appearance of the timeline as it adapts to reflect the new values.

You can drag and drop sequencer tracks up or down to re-order them. This doesn't affect any patching in the rack.

You can change the instrument associated with a sequencer track at any point by clicking the arrow next to its name and selecting from the list of available modules. This is useful if you want to see how a melody will sound played using a different instrument, but don't want to re-play or copy and paste the notes.

As you add more and more tracks, use the zoom controls to the left and right of the sequencer to get a better view. Also, use the small click box at the top right of the sequencer to maximise or minimize it.

Figure 5.4
Zoom out to get a better overall view of bigger projects

The left and right markers are crucial for recording loops and exporting material. Use alt + click on the timeline to set the position of the left marker and apple + click (Mac) or control + click (PC) to set the right. Alternatively, drag them to the desired position or enter position values in the toolbar.

Working with sequencer tracks

Material in the sequencer can be used in different ways. By material, we mean MIDI information. This can take the form of notes or other controller data such as velocity, sustain or automation. You can import MIDI files using the File > Import command as well as playing MIDI in yourself. Data on sequencer tracks displays in Arrange view as small red dots. The easiest way to manage sections of music is by

By detaching the sequencer window and then maximising it you can get a much better view of larger projects. To reattach, choose Window > Attach Sequencer Window.

using groups. When you have a melody or beat that needs to loop, draw around the notes using the pointer tool. Make sure you have snapping turned on, and set to snap to bar. The selected notes will go dark red. Then press apple + g (Mac) or control + g (PC) to have Reason group the notes together for easier handling.

Figure 5.5
Grouping notes makes them much easier to work with

Tip

By shift + clicking on the timeline you can set the end point of the project, which is displayed as a marker labeled E. To lengthen or shorten a project, pick up this marker and drag it to the right or left.

Some elements, like REX loops, are grouped automatically because they have a preset length. Here are some tips for grouping.

- When notes are grouped together they are much easier to copy, paste and delete. Reason lends itself to loop-based music (though you don't have to use loops of course), and working with 'blocks' of notes is much better than dealing with thousands of identical red dots.
- Reason assigns colours to groups as you create them. If you alter a loop in some way, its colour will change. This makes it much easier, say when building up a drum track, to see which groups are the same colour (and therefore the same pattern) and which are different (and therefore contain variations or automation data). When groups are colour coded like this it is easy to get a quick visual idea of how your track is shaping up.

Tip

To make an instrument play exactly the same notes as another instrument, simply copy the notes from one sequencer track to the other.

Figure 5.6
Colour coding makes groups easier to identify

- Groups can be picked up by the end and dragged left or right to alter their length. If snapping is turned on they will only drag to preset values like a bar or half a bar. With snapping off, they can be dragged to any point.
- Hold down alt and drag a group of notes left or right or to another sequencer track and an identical copy will be made.
- Select Edit > Group or Ungroup to perform these functions. Select Edit > Find Identical Groups with a group selected and Reason will hilghight all identical groups in the project.

Figure 5.7
The Find Identical Groups command is useful for locating identical sections of music

Elements of the Sequencer

Views

Key Edit

When you are in Edit mode (toggle using the button at the top left of the Sequencer) there are various different views that you can use. The most common is called the Key Lane. This simply displays the notes you have played as data, along with a keyboard for reference. This is where you perform detailed editing of MIDI notes. When you select a note it goes darker and gains a black dot to its right. Picking this dot up and dragging it will extend the length of the note. Notes can be dragged anywhere on a key editor to change the note that is played back. If you hold down alt (Mac) or Control (PC) and drag a note or group of notes they are duplicated. By drawing round groups of notes you can multiple select them and move them all together. Pressing backspace or selecting Edit > Delete or Cut will get rid of the notes.

In Edit mode, if you select different tracks from the track list on the left, the edit view on the right changes to display the notes for that track. If the track has additional types of control going on – say, patterns for a ReDrum or automation, those will automatically be displayed, meaning you don't have to switch different views on and off to see what a track contains. If you customise a view for a specific track, it is remembered for the next time you look at it.

Tip

With a group of notes selected, if you lengthen or shorten one note, all the others will be altered by the same amount.

Tip

In Key Edit mode, if you move the mouse over the vertical keyboard display the cursor changes to a tiny speaker. You can then play any of the notes using the mouse, to audition the sound without having to go to your MIDI keyboard.

Info

The Hand tool can be used to scroll up or down and left to right in any editor.

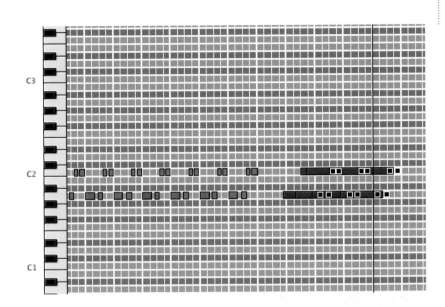

Figure 5.8 (left)
The Key Editor

Figure 5.9 (below)
The REX lane and Key lane both display REX loop information. Changes made in one are reflected in the other.

REX Lane Edit

The Dr.Rex player, ReDrum, NN-19 and NN-XT all support the playback of REX files to differing extents. Whenever a REX loop is loaded, it becomes available to edit in the REX lane. It also remains editable in the Key Editor. Activating Show REX Lane gives you access to the individual slices. The slices are numbered, and the longer a loop, the more slices it will have. If you have created your own REX files using ReCycle these numbers will correspond to the number of slices you chose.

The Key Editor and REX Lane editor should display the same patterns. This is because a REX file consists of slices of audio triggered by MIDI. Each note corresponds to a MIDI note on your keyboard and so slices 1 to 30 for example will equate to notes C1 up to almost C3 on the keyboard. If you have both open at the same time you can see that moving a note in one will affect the other. However, the loops (or groups of notes) exist independently on the timeline. If you change one, the others remain the same. This is useful for creating variations in REX loops without worrying about changing every loop.

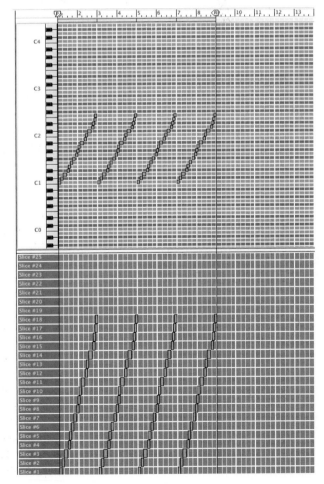

Drum Edit

Any ReDrum will have a Drum Edit lane available. This corresponds to each of the channels on the ReDrum, and the names of the loaded samples are displayed in the lane. Like with the Key Editor, you can audition any of these samples by clicking on their name in the edit lane.

The ReDrum is a bit different because it's a pattern device. This means you don't have to enter notes in the Drum or Key editors if you don't want to. By using Step Input mode and the pattern lane, you can sequence drums without playing MIDI keys. See the ReDrum chapter for more on this.

Figure 5.10
The ReDrum works with patterns as well as notes, via the Pattern lane

You can of course enter drum data the traditional way, by simply playing it in from a MIDI keyboard. In this case, notes appear in the Drum Editor and the Key Editor and can be manipulated in the same way as any other notes.

Figure 5.11
The Drum lane, where note data is shown in the same way as the other instruments

Velocity Lane

Every note has a velocity value, determining how loud it is. These range from zero to 127 – not actual decibels, but MIDI values. You can see the velocity of notes by activating the Velocity Lane, which should appear by default anyway. The darker the shade of red, the higher the velocity.

Use the pencil tool to edit the velocity of individual notes. Click above or below a note in the velocity lane to change the value. To create gradual changes, draw

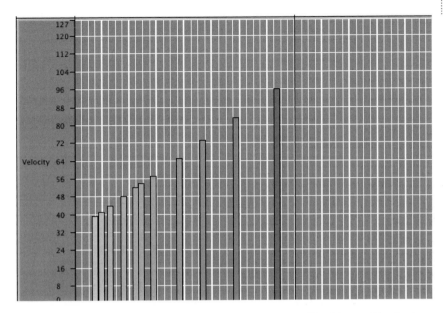

Figure 5.12
Create velocity ramps and edit velocity data
in the Velocity lane

from one side to the other whilst also going up or down. The Line tool is the best way to create steady velocity changes. Click and drag in the Velocity lane to create uniform changes. This is particularly useful for creating drum rolls as well as evening out natural variations in your playing which you may not want to be present.

If you multiple select notes and then hold down Shift when editing velocity values, only the notes you have selected will be affected. This is useful in places where there are many notes crowded together and you only want to edit certain ones by the same amount. For example, in a drum pattern let's say you wanted to make every other snare hit louder. Changing volume on the ReDrum would change every snare hit. Selecting every other beat in the velocity editor then using shift and the line tool would save you a lot of time.

Figure 5.13
Edit nonsequential notes' values by using
key presses when editing

Pattern Lane

Any pattern device like the ReDrum or Matrix can store a number of preset patterns, which can then be triggered at different points from the Sequencer. The Pattern Lane works not with MIDI notes but blocks which determine which sequence is played, and for how long. For more information on this see the Matrix section below, and the ReDrum chapter.

Figure 5.14
The Pattern lane

Tip

To delete a pattern you have to draw a shaded area around it and then press backspace or Edit > Delete. You can't select individual pattern events as you can with MIDI notes. To turn off pattern automation altogether for a track, select Edit > Clear Automation.

Controllers

Almost every parameter on every module can be controlled and automated. Parameter changes range from simple on / off controls to filter sweeps, effects amounts, LFO controls and so on. This is usually achieved by creating a sequencer track for the device (if it doesn't already have one) and then changing the parameters in realtime as you play and record. In Reason 3, automation can now be recorded on

Figure 5.15
Record automation on multiple channels at once

multiple tracks at the same time. Simply activate the red record button next to each track in the sequencer you want to automate. Obviously this works better it you have multiple MIDI control devices plugged in, as you can only do so much at once with the mouse.

To record multiple automation parameters using just the mouse, set up a loop over the section of music you want and use the red buttons to automation-enable the desired devices. Then as you play back and loop you can move between devices and alter parameters. Everything you have previously automated will continue to play back that automation as you record new changes in realtime, all without having to stop recording.

With so many parameters available for automation, a quick way of specifying one to view in edit mode is to hold Option (Mac) or Alt (PC) and click on it. This opens edit view and brings the automation subtrack for that parameter to the front. This saves a lot of time hunting for the relevant subtrack, especially if many are automated. This can also be done by Control (Mac) or right-clicking (PC) on a parameter and choosing Edit Automation from the contextual menu.

Figure 5.16
Quickly jump to the automation subtrack for any available control

Info

If you select Show Device Controllers in Edit View, every available parameter's subtrack will be shown. A more sensible idea is to click Show Controllers in Track, which only displays any currently automated parameters. Finally, the Controllers button gives you a menu from which to choose to display any of the available controller subtracks.

In Reason 3 it is possible to copy and paste automation between controller lanes in the Sequencer, for the same track or different tracks. This works using the usual copy or cut and then paste, when you have selected the target subtrack. This also works with multiple parameters using Shift to multiple select areas of data.

Figure 5.17
Copy and paste automation between tracks in Reason 3

Automation data can be dragged around the subtrack to move it. Rather than trying to recreate the same sweep or fade, just copy the automation from the subtrack. You can select it and then use Alt (Mac) or Control (PC) and drag to duplicate it.

The Matrix Pattern Sequencer

The Matrix pattern sequencer is sometimes overlooked but is actually a very powerful tool that complements Reason's main sequencer. The best way to think of it is as a sort of step sequencer – similar to old hardware sequencers like Roland Grooveboxes. It doesn't generate sound, but sends CV (control voltage) signal to CV inputs on other modules. It can transmit three types of CV data:

- Note CV, which controls the pitch of a note. The main part of the grid on a Matrix is for entering note data.
- Gate CV, which controls note on/off and level. This is important because without a note on and level value, a pitch value won't produce any sound. You need to tell a Matrix what note to play, at what level and for how long. The lower part of the grid is for entering gate CV.
- Curve CV, which is a more generic type of controller data to modulate other parameters such as filter, volume and pan.

The reason that the Matrix is so flexible is that it can control more or less any parameter. Most instruments and effects have a number of CV inputs to control different settings. Many also have sequencer control CV inputs. This is probably the

Figure 5.18
The Matrix is ideal for creating sequences of notes for electronic music

most common use for a Matrix – to build up sequences of notes. Reason lends itself to electronic and dance music, so you may want to create acid or techno synth sequences. As the program lacks a dedicated arpeggiator module, you can use the Matrix to achieve complex patterns without having to play them in by hand.

Working with the Matrix

If you select an instrument in the rack and then create a Matrix, it will automatically be routed to the sequencer control inputs of that instrument. If the module does not have these inputs, the Matrix will remain unconnected until you patch it manually.

Figure 5.19
Connect a Matrix as you would connect an insert effect, and its note and gate CV outputs are automatically connected

The Matrix can play independently of the main sequencer using its Run button. You can audition patterns without having to render them to the timeline. They remain 'virtual' within the Matrix. You can store up to 32 patterns in each Matrix sequencer. There are eight pattern slots and four banks. Switching between patterns is synchronized so the next one won't start playing until the last one has finished. This means no unexpected jumps.

Each of the 32 patterns stored can be completely different. Each can have a different length, resolution and octave setting. Each Matrix can only control a single voice in an instrument, but there's no limit to how many matrix modules you can create. Use the octave control on the left to move up and down the scale. A Matrix will always follow the master project tempo, but you can alter the resolution of the pattern using the knob on the right. Typically this might be 1/16.

To add swing to a pattern and make it feel less mechanical, activate the shuffle button on the Matrix. Set the amount of shuffle globally using the Pattern Shuffle knob on the Transport Panel. Shuffle on/off is stored separately with each pattern, so it can be on or off for any of the 32 patterns in a Matrix.

Figure 5.20
The Run button plays the Matrix independently of the main sequencer

Figure 5.21
The Resolution switch

Figure 5.22
The Shuffle controls

If you plug the outputs of a Matrix sequencer into other CV inputs such as filter, mod or pitch you can start to get some interesting sounds. For example, creating a sequence then connecting the Matrix to the OSC pitch and phase inputs on a Subtractor, then pressing Run on the Matrix and playing a MIDI note will produce a totally new sound.

Following from the above example, if you switch from key to curve mode on the Matrix and connect the curve CV output to, say, the filter res input on the synth, you start to further affect the

Figure 5.23
Create further variation in your sequences by connecting the curve CV output to the OSC pitch CV input on a synth.

Figure 5.24
Draw curve values by entering curve mode
on the Matrix

sound. A switch on the back of the Matrix lets you toggle between unipolar and bipolar modes. When drawing curve CV values, sometimes you need to go from plus into negative values. For example, when automating pan on the mixer. Fully to the top might represent a pan hard left and to the bottom, a pan hard right. In bipolar mode the centre line becomes zero. In unipolar mode the bottom line is zero.

Tip

When drawing data into the note or curve CV grids, hold down shift to draw smooth, gradual values.

Tip

Part of the fun of sequences is adding an element of randomization. With a pattern selected in a Matrix, you can choose from the Edit menu to shift a pattern around, alter it or randomize it completely. Also use this menu to cut, paste and clear patterns.

Tip

When drawing in gate CV in the lower part of the grid, hold the shift key to create tied rather than single notes. To permanently enable tied notes, press the Tie button. Now, pressing shift when drawing will enter single notes.

Info

The Spider CV Merger / Splitter can take CV signal generated by a Matrix and send it to multiple destinations, or combine CV signal from several places. Practical applications for this include having a single Matrix play the same pattern on several synths at once, or automating filters on a number of devices at the same time, in perfect sync.

Tip

Each pattern can be between 1 and 32 steps long. To quickly alter this value, click and hold on the step box at the top right, then drag the mouse up or down.

Figure 5.25
The Spider CV unit is the perfect partner for the Matrix

Recording Matrix data to sequencer tracks

After setting up all these different patterns, you do of course have to get them into the main sequencer in some way so Reason knows how to incorporate them into your track. There are several ways to do this, depending on how you like to work.

With the Matrix selected in the rack, and its associated sequencer track selected in the sequencer, select Edit > Copy Pattern to Track. This renders down the currently selected pattern to the sequencer. To copy another pattern, move the playhead, select the new pattern from the Matrix and repeat. A pattern must have note and level values present to be copied, otherwise nothing will happen. Remember to also move the L and R locators, as this is where Reason will put the sequencer data.

Figure 5.26
Copying Matrix patterns to sequencer note data

Once the data is in the main sequencer you can either drag and drop it to the sequencer track of another instrument to make it play back through that instrument, or re-assign the Matrix sequencer track to play back another module. The first option is probably easiest.

Figure 5.27
Dragging the Matrix notes to the synth's sequencer track to make it play the same sequence of notes

With the Matrix selected in the sequencer, play back the project whilst recording. Change the patterns in realtime as the track plays by pressing the pattern select buttons on the Matrix. Reason records these changes. Now when you play back, the matrix will swap patterns as you did when recording. The changes can be viewed and edited using the Pattern lane. The Matrix also gains a purple outline box to show that it has been automated.

Figure 5.28
Recording pattern changes in realtime

If you switch to Edit mode in the sequencer view, you will see that the Pattern lane for the Matrix has been activated. You will then see the patterns represented by blocks of colour on the timeline. Each new block corresponds to a pattern change. By using the dropdown menu in this lane to select one of the 32 patterns you can take the pen tool and draw in instances of the pattern. This is basically the same as recording in realtime, but gives you more of a graphical view. Remember a Matrix can only play one pattern at once, so they can't overlap.

Recording

A fter a couple of hours spent playing with Reason you will probably have created your first tune. As is sometimes the case with software, there are often several ways of achieving the same things, and you can choose the one that suits you best. For example, it can be easier when making electronic or dance music to enter note information by hand using the pen tool, as you can create sequences and patterns that would be impossible to play by hand. By using a sustain pedal with your MIDI keyboard you can achieve more realistic piano and string sequences. In fact most traditionally keyboard-based patches benefit from the addition of a sustain pedal. For more experienced keyboard players it is fairly essential to have one. If you don't have one, the Edit mode lets you draw in sustain by hand, as well as a number of other parameters such as velocity, pitch and even breath control. This is covered in more detail in the preceding chapter.

Figure 6.1
Edit mode allows you to draw sustain data in by hand, or edit it if it has already been recorded

If your MIDI keyboard has realtime controllers on it, Reason will read and remember any changes you make with them as it records. Reason 3 has the Remote system which allows you to control several devices from multiple keyboards or controllers at the same time, and record automation for them.

MIDI data exists independently of any instruments. Because of this, you can move or copy any notes in the sequencer to any track and have them played back by any instrument. This is useful for creating unusual passages – say, a piano part played back by a drum machine, and also for having several modules play exactly the same notes at the same time. At the other end of the scale, you can also import ready-made MIDI files created in other programs and simply reassign instruments to play them back.

Figure 6.2 (right)
Reason supports the import of MIDI files. You can re-assign instruments to play the tracks

MIDI information is basically a standard format, and so a MIDI file exported from one program should work in another. However, some programs will not support every parameter in the exported files. For instance, when exporting MIDI from Cubase SX to Reason, certain parts like VST instrument automation will not be translated, as there are no VST instruments in Reason.

MIDI files tend to contain note data but not Reason specific instrument data. If you import a MIDI file into Reason it will bring note data into the sequencer, as well as controller data like pitch bend, volume and mod wheel, but will not auto-

Figure 6.3
Importing a standard MIDI file into an empty project will bring note data and sequencer tracks but will not load up any instruments

matically load up the relevant modules and patches. If you are sharing files with other Reason users, use Reason song files rather than Standard MIDI files unless you specifically only need note or controller data to be sent.

As you create instruments in the rack, they appear as a list in the sequencer. In Reason 2.5, by selecting an instrument and clicking the 'In' column next to it, a MIDI plug icon appears and that instrument receives MIDI. In Reason 3, the track which has the keyboard icon lit is the one that will receive MIDI from the master keyboard. Other keyboards can be assigned to other modules, as described below.

Figure 6.4
The lit keyboard icon means MIDI input is being directed to that track

Info

Tempo changes in imported MIDI files are ignored.

Info

When you export a MIDI file from Reason, it will be of type 1. This means it contains one MIDI track for each track in Reason's sequencer. Track names and sequencer tempo are also included.

If you are playing loop-based rather than freeform music, setting the left and right markers and activating the loop button will cause Reason to cycle continuously between the two points. There are two record modes – replace and overdub. In replace mode, Reason will get to the end of a cycle, start the loop again and delete the existing notes as it goes over them. Overdub adds to the loop as it goes round again, keeping and playing back the original notes as you go over them. This is handy for building complex loops, and is the mode most commonly used in practice.

Figure 6.5
Overdub and replace record modes

Recording to a click track – at least until you have recorded a drum or rhythmic part for reference – will make your life much easier. Even if you are just improvising with a piano sound, if you capture a moment of genius it's much easier to then build the part into a song if it's been recorded in time with the tempo of the project. Use the click level knob under the click on/off button to alter the volume of the click. The click track plays a high note, then three lower ones. The high note signifies the first beat of the bar.

Figure 6.6
Recording to a click track is usually essential if you have no other rhythmic parts for reference

Info

If you are recording in a loop and you don't like what you just recorded, you don't have to stop playback and delete the notes. Leave play and record running and just hit backspace on the keyboard. All the notes on that track within the loop will be deleted so you can have another go without breaking your flow.

Quantizing

Even experienced musicians can find it difficult to play precisely in time with a mechanical click track for the duration of several bars. After you have recorded notes in, some of them may be slightly (or wildly) out of sync with the click. As MIDI information is just a set of instructions, it can be made to behave how you want. In this case, you want to pull the notes into alignment with the grid. This process is called quantizing. It's often easier to see the results of quantizing by switching to the Edit view, where the notes can be seen much more clearly. By selecting a quantize value (1/16 is often a safe bet) with your notes selected and pressing the quantize button, Reason will snap the notes to the nearest grid positions, bringing them into time. For more complex passages, more unusual quantize values are available.

Figure 6.7
It's easier to see the effects of quantizing
notes in Edit view

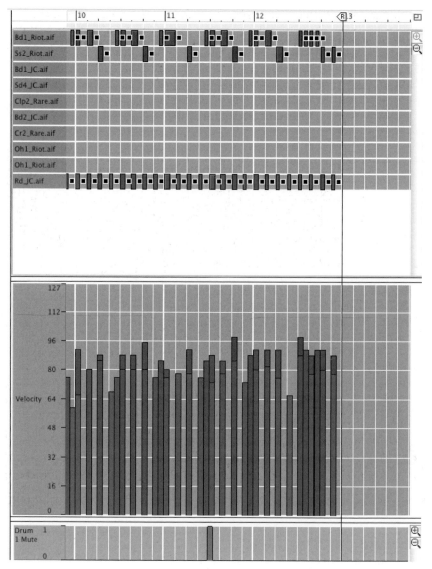

Figure 6.8
Use the Quantize Amount control to stay in
time but retain a natural feel to the music

A problem with quantizing is that it can make music, especially instruments like pianos, sound mechanical and a little too perfect. Luckily Reason has a Quantize Amount control, which lets you set just how strictly the notes are made to conform. Using a value of around 50 per cent balances out accuracy with a natural feel. There is also a button called Quantize Notes During Recording which if activated will snap notes to the grid as they are recorded. This can be useful for deliberately rhythmic parts like drums or synths, but can sound too regimented for other types of instrument. Remember you can always quantize after recording.

You can quantize individual notes or types of notes within a track. For example, say you have a ReDrum part that you've just played in by hand. You may want to quantize the hi-hats to a strict 1/16 setting, but the bass and snare to something a bit more fluid to maintain a funky feel. To do this, enter Edit mode and view the

Drum Lane (which should be visible by default). You can see the drum part arranged in a grid. Draw around the hi-hats to select them and then set the quantize value to 1/16 and press the quantize button. The hi-hats are snapped, but the other parts of the beat are not. Then you can draw around the other parts by track or as a group, and quantize them as you want, or not at all. Snapping to lower values may actually reduce the number of notes you hear by regimenting them to stick to a certain subdivision of beats. For example, quantizing to 1/2 will snap notes to every other beat.

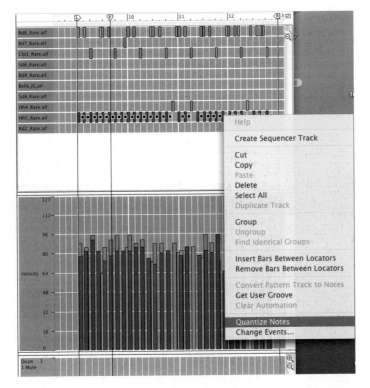

Figure 6.9
Quantize different notes using different values. In this example, just the hi-hats within a drum pattern

The Shuffle and Groove quantize settings apply snapping with a preset amount of swing in it. These can be useful for funky, shuffling beats which are still in time but less mechanical. Experimenting with them can produce interesting results.

Figure 6.10
The more unusual quantize presets allow for more natural 'swing' when snapping

You are not limited to preset quantize amounts. If you have played a sequence with a unique feel to it, or you have a REX file with a particular timing, and want to make other notes snap to that same timing, you can use the User Groove feature. Select the notes you want to 'extract' the groove from and select Edit > Get User Groove. In the Quantize Type menu, the User option is now available. Selecting different notes and quantizing them using the User setting will copy the feel of the original to the new notes. You can only store one User Groove at once, and it is not stored with the song file.

Figure 6.11
Extracting the Groove from a REX loop to use as a quantize preset for other notes

Change Events

There are some easier ways to edit certain parameters than just using the tools. In Arrange or Edit mode, by selecting notes on one or more tracks and selecting Edit > Change Events you can access some common editing functions. Transpose will shift the selected notes up or down by the desired number of semitones. This is very useful for creating variations in a song. For example, if you have created a great sec-

Figure 6.12
Change Events is a quick way to transpose multiple groups of notes

tion of music and then want it to switch from playing in C to E to create a middle eight, or a natural progression, just copy and paste the notes, select the new groups and transpose. Instantly, the whole section of the track is playing in a different key.

Remember that transposing essentially shifts notes on a grid. This is fine as long as the keys all have notes assigned to them. If you transpose a REX file or a ReDrum pattern in this way, you won't change the pitch of the notes but rather the order in which they are played back. On the upside, this can be used to create some drum variations that you would never otherwise have thought of. Transposing REX drum loops in this way causes them to start on beats other than the first, which is often better than the original loop, or at the very least, great for pattern variations. To properly transpose a REX loop in the traditional sense, use the transpose knob on the front of the Dr.Rex player.

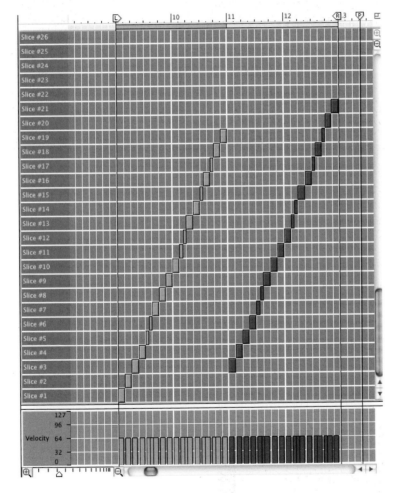

Figure 6.13
Transposing a REX lop from the Change Events menu will actually shift the order in which the notes play back

In the same way as Transpose, Velocity lets you alter velocity values for single or multiple notes. The Add field lets you enter a fixed value from 0 to 127, and the scale field lets you change velocities by a percentage. If you use the Add and Scale fields together you can change the dynamics of notes. For example, if you scale velocity to, say, 70% and also add an amount greater than ten or so, you can effec-

Figure 6.14

Figure 6.15

Tip

Alter Notes is great to use with REX loops, as it creates some variations without changing important properties like the feel of the loop.

tively compress the notes, in the sense that you will reduce the difference between the velocity values without lowering the average velocity (Figure 6.14).

The Scale Tempo control makes notes play back faster or slower. Use the x2 and /2 controls to quickly half or double the speed, or enter a value in the box. The Alter Notes control is a great way of adding variations to loops or parts. It randomizes the pitch, length and velocity of notes. The higher the value you enter, the greater the variation. It does however stay within the note range of the existing notes, so in effect it is shuffling what's already there around rather than placing notes at completely random pitches and velocities (Figure 6.15).

Locking Surfaces

A new feature in Reason 3 is the ability to assign specific controllers to individual devices in the rack. This is useful for playing live, but also for recording. There are many situations in which you might want to have more than one device recorded at the same time. Imagine for example that you have programmed a drumbeat over four or five minutes. You could then set up multiple keyboards, locked to devices and several people could use the system at the same time, and the results of controlling the modules recorded as you went along. Or if it was just you, set up a controller locked to the mixer and another as a master keyboard. Now you can have control over levels, mute and solo in the mixer, as well as being able to play any instrument by directing MIDI to it in the sequencer.

Surface Locking

If you have specified a master keyboard, it cannot be locked to a device. You can however choose to Use No Master Keyboard in the preferences. If you do this, you will be able to lock it to a device and tweak the controls, but not play it using the keys. Information about locked devices is saved with your song file.

Figure 6.16
Choose whether or not to use a master MIDI keyboard

A number of control surfaces can be locked to the same device, but each can only be locked to one device at a time. If the Reason module has more controls than your controller, say, the mixer for example, you can assign more than one controller to it and customise the setup so that between the controllers, all the parameters on the mixer can be used in realtime.

Access surface locking controls either by selecting Options > Surface Locking, or by control + clicking (Mac) or right-clicking (PC) on a device and selecting the Lock to option. Remember that if you only have one keyboard and have specified it to be the master, this option will not appear in the contextual menu. You can unlock a device in the same way as locking it.

Figure 6.17

Remote Override

A feature of this realtime control system is the ability to customise remote control maps. This is especially useful if you don't have a fully-featured USB controller, but rather a more generic MIDI keyboard with few or no realtime control knobs or sliders. Here are some things to know about this mode.

Access it either by selecting Options > Remote Override Edit Mode or control + click (Mac) or right click (PC) on a parameter and selecting Edit Remote Override Mapping

Figure 6.18
Remote Override Edit mode, for assigning controllers

Figure 6.19
A module displaying which of its parameters can be controlled in realtime

Accessed from the Options menu, modules are greyed out and the one you select gets highlighted. Parameters that can be controlled are shown using blue arrows. Double-click a parameter to activate MIDI learn. Move the control or note you wish to map and a tooltip appears to tell you it's been successfully assigned.

Accessed via the contextual menu, you get a more conventional MIDI learn window, from where you can assign controls in the more traditional way. On most modules, patch select buttons can be controlled, meaning a key press can cycle between patches.

If you use a key on the keyboard to assign to a parameter, it will change values between zero and 100 per cent – like an on/off button. So for example, a fader on the mixer can be set to zero or full using a key press. As long as you remember what triggers what, you could set up a basic keyboard just to control channels on/off in the mixer. Using masking tape on the keys with simple instructions is a good way to set up a controller in this way.

You can copy and paste Remote Overrides between devices of the same type. In Remote Override Edit mode you can choose a device with mappings and use the Edit menu to copy and paste the mappings to another device – e.g from ReDrum to

Info

You cannot map the same key or controller to more than one parameter.

Tip

Remove remote overrides in the same way as you assign them, by control or right clicking.

Figure 6.20
The contextual menu brings up a MIDI learn window

Tip

Pressing the escape key will instantly jump you out of Remote Override Edit mode.

ReDrum, or Dr.Rex to Dr.Rex. If pasting to the same project you are prompted to choose which of the two you want to have the mappings, as the same keys can't be mapped to more than one device. If you're pasting to a different project, there's no problem.

Figure 6.21
Remote control maps can be pasted between devices within a project, but if they conflict you have to choose one or the other

If you select Options > Additional Remote Overrides, you can assign some system-specific commands to controllers or keys. Various parameters like undo / redo, select next / previous track, go to locators and so on can be assigned. This is particularly useful in a live or live recording situation, as it won't break your flow or cause you to have to come back to the mouse and the keyboard to perform these tasks.

Tip

In Remote Override Edit Mode you can clear all mappings for a device in a single go by selecting it and choosing Clear from the Edit menu.

Figure 6.22
Additional Remote Overrides let you perform some system tasks from a MIDI controller

Tip

Standard Remote mapping for supported control surfaces is always available in Reason. If you create a custom setup for your unsupported kit, it's best to save it as a template containing the devices and mappings but no sequencer data so the controls will be available every time you open it. Remember to always re-save it as a different filename.

Keyboard Control

This function is a bit like Remote, only it works using the computer's keyboard, and can only be used to toggle things on or off, or values between zero and 100 per cent. It involves no MIDI data, just commands. It's sort of an extension of Reason's other key commands for saving, undoing and that sort of thing. To switch it on, choose Options > Enable keyboard Control. To assign keys, either enter Keyboard Control Edit Mode from the same menu, or right-click (PC) or control-click (Mac) on a parameter. Assigning commands is then done in the same way as with Remote, only the arrows are yellow. There is no crossover between Remote and Keyboard control, as one uses MIDI and the other does not. It works using something like the MIDI learn function, only with key presses.

Figure 6.23

Keyboard Control mode lets you assign certain commands to your computer keyboard

There are several uses for this:

- Setting up the numeric keys 1 to 0 to solo mixer channels.
- Assigning a row of keys to mute faders on the mixer.
- Setting up the numeric keypad to switch between patterns on a Matrix or a ReDrum.
- Assigning a key command to switch the mod wheel on a sampler from zero to full.
- Bypassing an effect with a key press

Basically, any parameter that comes up with a yellow arrow in Keyboard Control Edit mode can be assigned a key command. This is yet another way for you to customise Reason.

Using your own samples

Reason doesn't have a feature to record audio directly in, but that doesn't mean you can't use your own sounds. The NN-19 and NN-XT samplers both have two file load buttons. The first is to select patches designed for the module, but the second will load raw .WAV or AIFF audio files which can be played from the MIDI keyboard. Because they are individual samples they will get higher and faster as you

Figure 6.24
The samplers and drum machine in Reason
are able to load any audio file you have
recorded in another program

go up the keyboard, and lower and slower as you go down. Sometimes this is desirable, sometimes not, but it does mean that you can use your own loops. In a typical example you might record a guitar riff or a vocal into a wave editing package like Sound Forge or Peak then export it as an audio file. By loading this into one of Reason's samplers you can use it in your song. The sound doesn't go into the sequencer, rather a MIDI note is recorded to trigger the sample, just like with real hardware samplers. The NN-XT and ReDrum are able to load samples in more advanced ways. See their specific chapters for more on this.

Automation

Automation used to be a feature only of high-end studio hardware. Happily, it's now available to a much wider audience including Reason users. The concept is simple – record the movement of controls as you move them. Then when you play back, the controls move by themselves. Software affords us huge possibilities on this front, as it tends to be more flexible than hardware.

One of the most common types of automation is mixer automation. You can use this to make faders, pan and EQ controls, for example, move by themselves. Automating a mix makes creating interesting tracks much easier. For instance, you may have a piano line that plays loud in the chorus but quietly during the verse. Rather than duplicating parts onto different tracks, just automate the fader at the right point so that the volume increases and decreases by itself. The same principle applies to automating anything (Figure 6.25).

Info

In theory you can create entire tracks by just using your own samples.

Figure 6.25
An automated mixer, displaying green boxes around controls that have been recorded

Before you record automation it's a good idea to set a controller to the value it's supposed to have when it's not being automated. This is because Reason takes this to be its 'static' value and as soon as you start recording, will insert this value throughout the song for that parameter. You can see this graphically if you view the automation subtrack in Edit mode. To prevent controls from jumping around unexpectedly, this is a good move. For example, to create a fade out, make sure the fader is at its normal value before you start to automate the fade out. Reason will then know that at every point previous to the start of the fade, the fader should be at that original value.

Figure 6.26
Reason inserts values as soon as you start automating a control

If a device is to be automated, it must have a track in the sequencer. Instruments should automatically have one, but mixers and effects will not. Select the mixer and choose Create > Sequencer Track, then assign the mixer to it using the icon box in the sequencer track view. Alternatively, right-click (PC) or control-

Figure 6.27
Create a sequencer track if you want to automate non-instrument devices

click (Mac) on the mixer and select Create > Sequencer Track for Mixer. All devices can be assigned sequencer tracks in this way, except devices with no realtime controls such as the two Spider devices, the Hardware Interface and the ReBirth input machine.

Automation is recorded by pressing play and record, and using the controls you want to automate. In Reason 2.5 the track that is to be automated must have the MIDI icon next to it in the sequencer. In Reason 3, automation can be recorded on multiple tracks at once. Simply press the red record button for every track you want to automate. This is ideal if you take advantage of the multiple controller support and have several people playing the system at once. All their controller movements will be recorded.

Tip

Automation drawn by hand will obey the snapping rules if snapping is on. This is useful for creating automated events that are perfectly in time — say, changing filter amounts over a bar with one change every beat. Alternatively, deactivate snapping and you have total freedom to draw unrestricted.

Figure 6.28
Recording automation on several tracks at once

If you have automated a parameter and want to redo or change it, you can use the tools in Edit mode. Alternatively, go back over the same section whilst recording and 'grab' the controller at any point. Reason will overwrite the automation from the point you start to change it. The Punched In LED on the Transport Panel will light up to signify that you have done this (Figure 6.29).

You can still 'grab' a controller at any point, even if it has been automated, to temporarily regain control of it. Imagine you have programmed a fade but decide on the spur of the moment to drop the channel straight out or straight in. You don't have to be recording, and if you move that controller, its automation will be disabled for as long as Reason plays back. As soon as you stop and start playback, automation is re-enabled.

Figure 6.29
Automation Punched In LED

Tip

Once a parameter has been automated it gets a green box around it. This stays even when Reason isn't playing, and makes it easy to quickly see what has been automated at a glance.

With a bit of clever automation you can create much more professional sound-ing tracks, more interesting synth sounds and effects. If you control-click or right-click on a parameter you can select Edit Automation, which will transfer the sequencer view straight to the automation subtrack for that parameter. If you alt-click (Mac) or control-click (PC) on a parameter, Reason will jump straight to its automation subtrack.

The Combinator

This module, introduced in Reason 3 is a sort of 'shell' within which you can build chains of other devices. It isn't an effect or an instrument, but rather a tool to help you get more out of the other modules. It saves and loads setups in its own file format with the suffix .cmb. Think of it sort of like a rack within the rack. You can have as many Combinators as your CPU can handle, and they come in two basic forms. Instrument combis can contain any combination of instruments, effects and mixers. Effect combis only contain effects units and are used to process rather than generate sound.

Figure 7.1
An instrument combi

Figure 7.2
An effect combi

The most obvious applications for the Combinator are threefold. Firstly, for instant recall of instrument / effect combos that you use a lot. Let's say that you have a favourite piano sound with reverb, compression and EQ on it, or a synth patch that sounds great through six Scream boxes. By building it once and saving as a combi patch, it's always available at the click of a button. No more re-building effects chains or copying and pasting from template songs.

Figure 7.3

Create a Combinator by either selecting from the Create menu or by selecting two or more modules in the rack using multiple (shift) select and then selecting Combine from the Edit menu. You can also find this option if you right-click or control-click to bring up the contextual menu with multiple modules selected (Figure 7.4).

You can't create a Combinator within another Combinator, or place one inside another by any means! However, if you drag and drop or copy / paste one into another, the devices from the one being copied are uncombined and re-combined within the target Combinator, after its existing modules. Hold shift to ensure auto-routing.

If you choose to create a device by browsing patches you can call any device up from the Browser window. As you browse for Combinator patches, they are loaded so you can play them from the Browser, and information about all modules inside the combi is displayed (Figure 7.5).

Details

Patch Type: Combinator
    Size: 58.84 MB (uncompressed)
Devices: Line Mixer 6:2, Spider Audio, RV7000, RV7000,
         NN-XT Sampler

If you use the up and down arrow keys on the keyboard you can quickly select different modules in the rack. This takes account of modules within a Combinator, and will 'jump' you inside one when you get to it.

The way to add devices to a Combi is to click in the space at the bottom of it, causing the red insertion line to appear. When this is lit, any device you create will be created inside the combi.

Figure 7.6
The red line means any devices you create will be placed inside the Combinator

You can drag and drop devices from anywhere in the rack into a combi by dragging their handles – the parts attached to the rack - into the combi.

Figure 7.7
Re-order devices in a combi by dragging their end handles

Be aware that when you do this, their original patch connections to the main mixer remain intact. Either manually re-patch them or do the following. As you drag the devices into the combi, hold the shift key and they will be re-routed to inside the combi. If you hold option (Mac) or alt (PC) as you drag the devices, they are copied rather than moved. You can drag devices within a combi to re-order them. The Combinator itself can be moved around the rack like any device.

Tip

Although a Combinator lets you play all the modules within it at the same time, by selecting the Out menu in its sequencer track you can direct MIDI to any of the modules within a combi.

Info

It's fairly essential to create a line mixer or even a ReMix as your first step when making a combi. If you just start to add instruments, only the first instrument will have its outputs sent to the main mixer. If you create a mixer and then add the instruments, their outputs are routed to that mixer, and the summed output is sent to the main mixer. Basically if you don't do this, you'll only hear the output of the first instrument you create! (Figure 7.8)

The second thing the Combinator is good at is making huge sounds. By layering up multiple instruments and effects within a single combi you can play them all at the same time. Layering sounds up in this way it's much easier to create new and massive patches, as big as your CPU will allow. You can for example create lush orchestral sounds by layering up pianos, strings, reverbs and horns all into a single combi. Or, mix different synth modules and effects to create complex electronic sounds.

Figure 7.9
Create very complex layered instruments and manage them easily

For really cool sounds, you can add pattern devices to a combi. So, by adding a Matrix or a ReDrum and pressing the Run Pattern Devices button, the sequence will play, but only when you press keys. Otherwise it won't make any sound. The sound will be synced to tempo! This is an excellent way of playing arpeggiated sounds and being sure they will stay in time. It also makes you look like a real pro!

Figure 7.10
Use pattern devices within a combi and you can play sequences independently of the main sequencer

In this way, using a couple of control surfaces or keyboards you could do an entire performance without having any data in the main sequencer at all. By further customising the combi and mapping some pads or keys to mutes, pattern changes and so on you can play an entire track, plus variations, from within one Combinator. Remember that each Matrix can store four banks each of eight patterns so there are 32 possible pattern variations within each one. And then remember also that you can have a number of people with controllers locked to separate Combinators, and the vast possibilities for live performance become apparent (Figure 7.11).

The way to manage combis is by using the programmer window. Press the Show Programmer and Show Devices buttons on the Combinator. For each device within a combi you can assign the four knobs and buttons on the front of the Combinator to perform a different task. Do this by opening the Programmer window, selecting the module you wish to control and then selecting from the list of available controls for rotary knobs 1-4 and buttons 1-4. This is incredibly useful because it means you can make one control do several things at the same time. For example, assigning rotary 1 to control cutoff knobs on four synths will create a sort of master cutoff control, letting you move them all at once. In another example, a button could be made to control multiple effect on/off buttons, letting you punch groups of effects in or out at the same time (Figure 7.12).

Figure 7.11
Map control devices to a Combinator and get control over the modules within it

Figure 7.12
The programmer window lets you customise the actions of the front panel controls

Info

You can rename the controls on the front of a Combinator to make life easier if you have assigned custom actions to them (Figure 7.13).

An easy way to split instruments over the keyboard is to open the combi Programmer window and for each instrument, define a key range. This section is contextual, so you get a different view depending on which instrument you select. Drag the key range slider for each instrument to set its boundaries. Remember, only instruments can be split, not effects.

Figure 7.14
Define key ranges to split sounds over the keyboard

You can use the keyboard to audition selected instrument devices by pressing Option (Mac) or Alt (Windows) and clicking on the keys. This is really useful for playing live. You may for example want to put a bass at the bottom end, piano in the middle and drums at the top of the keyboard. Easy to do by splitting the keyboard into zones. There are some great preset combis included in Reason to try out.

Info

Quickly mute effects within a combi by pressing the Bypass All FX button (Figure 7.15).

By selecting Edit > Select Backdrop with a Combinator selected, or right / control-clicking on it and selecting the same option, you can choose a custom backdrop for the Combinator. This is a first for Reason – you can actually choose any image of your own to use. There are templates supplied – images should be 754x138 pixels and jpeg format. By using the template and changing it in Photoshop you can create your own labels for buttons and any other customisations (Figure 7.16).

With a little practice and time spent setting up you can build some great combis for instant recall. They are particularly useful for playing live, as you can create custom setups, and then have multiple people playing different Combinators in realtime by locking controllers to them.

The NN-19 Sampler

When looking at Reason's instruments we're not going to do a blow-by-blow explanation of all the features. That can be found in the manual. Instead we're going to look at things you may not have known, tips for achieving certain common sorts of task and hidden secrets. There's a certain amount of overlap between the workings of many of the instrument modules. For example, the way they load patches, the way synthesis controls work on the synths, filter and envelope sections and so on. For this reason, these will only be mentioned when they are of particular significance to a tip or trick for the instrument in question, and not mentioned once for every module.

Reason doesn't record audio in, but there are certain ways around that. The most obvious is to ReWire it together with another sequencer. Alternatively, use a wave editor like Peak, Acid, Sound Forge or something similar to record audio in, then cut it to the right length and use it in one of Reason's sampling modules. The NN-19, NN-XT and ReDrum are all able to import audio samples in various formats. The safest bet is to stick with AIFF or WAV files for maximum compatibility, although SoundFont files are supported too. Remember that the NN-19 is a sample player, not a recorder.

The NN-19 sampler patches that are in the Factory Soundbank contain all the necessary information relevant to that patch. A sampler patch refers to one or more audio files contained within the ReFill. Most sampler patches here are based on multisampled instruments. For example, if you load up a piano in an NN-19, the sampler loads a number of audio samples, probably more than one for each note to account for different velocities (so that playing a key harder or softer will produce different types of sound). It also maps these samples across the keyboard and makes any filter, velocity or envelope settings that have been saved as part of the patch. When you save patches, this information is all stored too.

Figure 8.1
A sampler patch contains links to the audio files plus any other relevant settings

The NN-19 can be used in two main ways – loading patches or loading samples. The file browser button on the left lets you open patches – ready-made instruments, mapped over the keyboard. It also lets you load REX files, which are automatically mapped in sequence over as many keys as the loop has slices. The file browser button in the middle lets you browse for individual audio samples, including those that make up the patches, and also REX files.

Figure 8.2
The NN-19 can load sampler patches and individual audio samples

You can load any of the individual slices of a REX file into an NN-19.

Info

There's an interesting way to make an NN-19 play back a REX loop based on its original form. Load an NN-19 and load the REX loop. Now create a REX player and load the same loop into it. Use its To Track button to place the MIDI notes on its sequencer track. Then drag these notes to the sequencer track for the NN-19 and delete the REX player. The NN-19 will now play the REX loop based on the original REX note data. You MUST load the REX loop into the NN-19 using the patch browser button for this to work. You can multiple-load the slices using the file browser button and repeat this trick for some interesting runs of notes when you paste the sequencer data (Figures 8.3 and 8.4).

Figure 8.3
Make an NN-19 play back a REX loop with its original rhythm

Figure 8.4
Load multiple REX slices into the sampler for greater control over individual parts of the loop

Info

When you browse for samples, use the Autoplay feature in the browser to let you hear them, When you play the keyboard you'll be able to audition the sounds without actually loading them into the rack.

When you have loaded a sample, you can start to alter its parameters using the main window on the NN-19. The whole point about samplers is that you can change the way audio is played back without altering the original audio file on your hard drive. Here is how you could incorporate some of your own recorded material into a Reason song without using ReWire.

Use your own samples

Record your sound in a wave editing package. There are lots of cheap and even free ones available. If it is rhythmic in any way, record it to a click track. This is essential for syncing it up later in Reason. You can even use a real metronome, just as long as it's in time. Cut the file into a loop so that it starts and ends at points which allow it to loop perfectly. If the file is a 'hit' and isn't going to be looped, the start point is much more important than the end point.

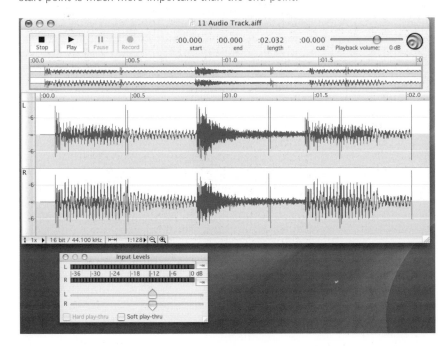

Figure 8.5
Use a wave editing package to record your own audio in

Save the file somewhere, naming it sensibly. Then use the middle file button on an NN-19 to find it and load it. Its root key gets mapped to C3 on your keyboard. This is the key that you press to trigger the sample as it was originally recorded. If you load a single sample, it will be mapped across the entire keyboard. If you play lower and higher keys, the sample will play back at different speeds and pitches.

Figure 8.6
Load individual samples using the file browser button

Let's say you have loaded a drum loop. If it has been recorded to a click but you don't know its tempo, just activate the click track and attempt to play the sample in time with it. By altering the project's tempo so that the loop plays in time with the click you can make it sync properly. Of course this works best if you don't already have loads of material in the sequencer – if you are using the loop as the starting point for a track rather than adding it to an existing track. If in doubt, set up a four-bar loop and play the sample in once at the start of each bar. Quantize to Bar to make sure it snaps. You could also turn Forward looping on for the sample and just play it once at the very start of the loop. Then, adjust the song's tempo until the loop syncs properly. If your loop hasn't been recorded to a click this step will be very difficult. It also helps greatly if the sample starts at the very beginning of the audio file – if there isn't any silence before the sound comes in.

Figure 8.7
Bring your own loops in and match them to the song's tempo by setting up a loop and changing the tempo until it fits

Record the track by holding the key or drawing with the pen tool in the Edit window. Make sure the note starts precisely at the start of a bar. You may need to quantize it to ensure this happens. If your sample is set to loop forwards, you can press the note at the beginning of the bar and then hold it until the end. This will count as one note but will trigger the sample several times. Remember when you play back that in order to trigger the sample the play head must run over the start of the note. If you start it from halfway through the note, nothing will happen.

If you are working with a single hit rather than a loop, you don't need to worry about looping. A popular way of making samples 'stutter' is to play them repeatedly with one finger on the keyboard and end up holding the note so the whole sample plays.

Info

There are three modes for looping samples – Off, Forward and Forward-Backward. The most useful is Forward. Provided you have created your sample so that it loops seamlessly, you can have your loop playing in sync all the way through the track.

Figure 8.8
Looping forwards is a good way of repeating a sample without it having to be played manually many times.

Info

A really useful way of auditioning samples without using the keyboard is to option (Mac) or alt (PC) click on the keyboard in the NN-19's window and then choose a note (Figure 8.9).

Info

Samples can be fine-tuned and have their volume altered using the controls under the NN-19's window.

To load several samples into the same sampler, multiple-select them in the browser. Then, by selecting Edit > Split Key Zone you can start to divide the keyboard up into separate zones, which cannot overlap.

Figure 8.10

Use the Sample knob below to assign each sample to each key zone. You can also pick up the little light blue dividers and drag them around to move the key zones. You can also do this by using the High and Low Key knobs. If your samples contain root key information, you can use the Automap Samples feature from the Edit menu to automatically place all samples in a sampler correctly on the keyboard according to its root note.

Figure 8.11
Automapping samples helps to assign them key ranges based on their root key information, if they have it

There are several other useful things on the front panel of the NN-19 that can help you to be more creative. Here are some ideas.

The Front Panel

The Sample Start knob lets you set a start point for the sample other than the actual start of the file. This can be really useful if, say, there is a breath before a vocal begins, or if there is a glitch at the start of a sound. This control can be used to effectively mute them without changing the sample itself.

Figure 8.12

Use the Pitch controls to make small or large changes to the sample's pitch. Using the octave control can give you some interesting effects.

The filter controls – especially the frequency slider – are great when you automate them, giving some classic filter sweep effects.

Figure 8.13

You can achieve some really good modulation effects by using the LFO controls on the NN-19. Take a normal sound like a guitar or a piano patch. Then Switch on Sync in the LFO (this is optional but it helps) and raise the amount and rate to somewhere between 50 and 100%. Choose a wave type from the list of six. Now play back. Using the Destination button you can send the mod to osc, filter or pan. Sent to osc, you end up with some cool space effects. A piano is turned into a ray gun sound when you do this. Select filter and provided the filter frequency control is set to something other than full, you get a wah wah or tremelo effect. Set to Pan, you get a nice, almost arpeggiator effect. The results vary depending on the settings you make.

By using the Velocity control section you can make sounds harder or softer. Also, try setting the polyphony to one, then switch the Key Mode to Legato. If you play one note and then play another without releasing the first one, you get an interesting synth-like effect where the subsequent notes have very little attack.

The Voice Spread controls can add a sense of stereo width to your tracks. The three modes will move the pan value of the sound as you play from left to right on the keyboard. Switch polyphony up to be able to play more notes at the same time if you need to.

Figure 8.14
Use the LFO controls to mangle ordinary sounds into totally different ones

Figure 8.15

Remember that an NN-19 can be played using a Matrix for some interesting sequence effects, just like any other module. It's particularly useful for creating runs of notes or arpeggiated sequences.

Figure 8.16
The Matrix sequencer can play the NN-19 if you enter data into it

The ReDrum

M odelled partly on vintage, step-based drum machines, the ReDrum combines the strengths of step sequencing with the flexibility of software. That flexibility includes the fact that you can mix and match elements of a drum kit, build your own and automate it just like any other instrument in Reason.

There are several ways to use a ReDrum. By loading patches from the file browser button at the bottom left you can load proprietary .drp patches, which call up drum samples into each of the ten channels on the ReDrum.

Name	Modified	Size
Chemical Kit 01.drp	1/12/2005	7 kB
Chemical Kit 02.drp	1/12/2005	7 kB
Chemical Kit 03.drp	1/12/2005	7 kB
Chemical Kit 04.drp	1/12/2005	7 kB
Chemical Kit 05.drp	1/12/2005	7 kB
Chemical Kit 06.drp	1/12/2005	7 kB
Chemical Kit 07.drp	1/12/2005	7 kB
Chemical Kit 08.drp	1/12/2005	7 kB
Chemical Kit 09.drp	1/12/2005	7 kB
Chemical Kit 10.drp	1/12/2005	7 kB

(Chemical Kits / Show: Redrum patches)

Figure 9.1
Proprietary ReDrum patches

Or, you can use the file select button on each channel to load any sample you like into each channel. You can mix and match too. Loaded a Reason drum kit but don't like the snare? Change it for one of your own by using the browser on that particular channel. In fact, there's nothing to stop you loading ten snares into a module and just playing those. Or eight horn stabs and a cymbal – it's up to you (Figure 9.2).

Figure 9.2
Use your own samples in any ReDrum channel. They don't have to be drum samples if you don't want them to be

Tip

You don't have to load drum samples into the ReDrum. Try loading sound fx or instrument hits, mixing and matching kits and effects in the channels. When you play them back from the keyboard you'll get some weird and wonderful results.

Figure 9.3
Each channel has independent audio controls

Each channel has its own set of audio controls. This means you can edit the sound of each constituent part of your drum loop. For example, the bass drum might need to be lowered in pitch and raised in volume. Or the hats might need panning. All this can be done without affecting the other channels in the ReDrum. This is also interesting if you load a REX file into a ReDrum. By loading the slices into channels separately you can gain control over the sound of each slice really easily and then assemble them into entirely new patterns. The sound loaded into each channel can be auditioned, muted or soloed by using the three buttons at the very top of it. It's also easy to make drum sounds snappier by reducing their length using the Length knob.

Info

By using the Level and Velocity controls on each drum channel you can effectively sub-mix a kit before it is sent to the mixer. This saves you having to try to even out the drums too much with compressors and EQ. There's also a Master Level control at the top left.

Each channel has two effect send knobs near the top of it, corresponding to the first two send effects attached to the main mixer. Using these is a good way of effecting parts of a drum pattern but not others. For example, applying reverb to the snare but not the bass drum. You can even apply effects only to certain snare beats (for example) by having the same snare loaded into two channels, one playing most of the way through the pattern but the second playing periodically and through the effect.

Figure 9.4
Effect drum kit elements separately using the effects sends on each channel

Step recording

The two record modes – step and normal sequencer – are covered in detail in the manual. However there are some useful tricks to be found when recording.

Everything is contextual, so the drum channel that is selected is the one that will be controlled by the 16 step buttons. The Select button lights up for the active channel, and only one can be selected at once.

You can switch each pattern up to a total of 64 steps. If you go beyond 16, you have to use the Edit Steps switch to make the visible step buttons correspond to the additional steps beyond 16 that you have added. You can of course shorten a pattern, in which case any steps programmed after will simply not play back.

Figure 9.5

Figure 9.6
Work with up to 64 steps, using the Edit Steps knob to access them all

If you're working in step mode you have to have the Enable Pattern Section button activated. Use the Run control to stop and start patterns. You can play the ReDrum patterns without ever actually starting the main sequencer, as it has its own sequencer in it. When you use the pattern select buttons and banks to choose new patterns, Reason waits until the current one has finished playing before mov-

Figure 9.7

Press a ReDrum Run button and hear it
without starting the main sequencer

ing on to the next. This is great for playing it live as it means you can flip between patterns without fear of slipping out of sync.

Each step can have a hard, medium or soft dynamic applied to it to create more natural variations in the dynamics of a pattern. Either select the step and alter the setting, or hold down shift while clicking to apply a hard dynamic.

Figure 9.8

The Shuffle control will introduce a more natural 'swing' to the pattern. The amount of swing is set globally, using the Pattern Shuffle knob on the Transport Panel. Use with care, as it can often wildly change the feel of a pattern, and not always for the better.

The Resolution control lets you alter the subdivisions of beats to which the ReDrum is locked. 1/16 is the normal setting. 1/32 can be good for Drum and Bass, and other settings like 1/64 or 1/128 let you program drum rolls and fills. The more precise the resolution, the more intricate the beats you can program.

Figure 9.9

Alter the resolution to create more complex
patterns

You can simulate double drum hits by using the Flam control. Activate Flam and then set the amount and click the LED above each step you want to have flam. A little usually works better than a lot, and it will take a bit of practice to get it sounding really natural. This is also a good way of creating double bass drum kicks, very close together.

Figure 9.10
The Flam control helps to create doubled-up drum effects

Here is a good way of creating a convincing snare 'double hit'. Identify the snare beat you want and then insert another one directly before it, with its dynamic set to soft. Then apply a Flam value of around 55 to that quieter snare hit. Voila... a short drum fill.

Each of the ten channels on the ReDrum has a separate audio L and R out, as well as CV in and out. This makes it incredibly versatile. Although you might normally just send the summed stereo output to the mixer, you can separate off some or all of the channels and process them independently. Imagine – you could build amazing drum kits by sending each channel to a separate mixer channel, where you apply different effects, pan and automated levels to each one. If you use up every channel on one ReMix, just create another.

Figure 9.11
Route some or all of the ten drum channels out and process them independently, for amazing versatility

Figure 9.12

A good way to create stereo space in a ReDrum is to duplicate, say, a hi-hat track and pan one channel left and one right.

The Edit menu gains some useful items when you select a ReDrum. There are a multitude of ways to modify the patterns you create, which saves you time programming variations. The most useful are :

- Cut, Copy, Paste and Clear pattern. Save time when varying patterns by copying and pasting patterns to a new slot and making minor changes.
- Shift Pattern and Shift Drum. These move notes for a pattern or drum channel to the left or right. Again, great for creating variations.
- Randomize Pattern and Drum will create a totally new arrangement for either the whole pattern or just the selected drum channel. Variations, here we come!
- Alter Pattern and Drum make changes by re-allocating the current notes to the drum sounds at random. This is less chaotic than simply randomizing them.

Info

There's an interesting feature whereby if you select Channel 8&9 Exclusive on a ReDrum, the sound from one will automatically silence the other. This is useful for tasks like making sure an open hi-hat cuts of a closed one, as you get in real life.

Tip

You will find that keys C2 to E3 on your keyboard actually mute the drum channels on a ReDrum. This is an interesting way of creating drum patterns – by having loads of drum hits playing, and selectively muting them on the fly by using the keyboard. The results are usually chaotic...

Sequencer recording

If you deactivate the Enable Pattern Section button, the ReDrum works like a normal sound module and you can play notes in by hand from the MIDI keyboard. Again, this is best done to a click track and quantized afterwards. If you have recorded a drum pattern in step mode you can convert it to MIDI notes by selecting the required pattern on the ReDrum and choosing Copy Pattern to Track.

Figure 9.13 (right)

The notes will then be inserted between the left and right locators. This works for any pattern you select, but be aware that if you try to copy more than one pattern to the same area on the sequencer, both sets of notes will co-exist at the same point, which can get very cluttered. One upside of copying notes like this is that it gives you a much clearer view of what's being played.

Figure 9.14
Copy drum patterns to the sequencer from the ReDrum

Notes can be placed in the Key lane, Drum lane and REX lane for a ReDrum, which gets a bit busy sometimes. If you have recorded some patterns using step mode, a good way to put those into the sequencer is using the Pattern lane. Here are some things to know about programming patterns in the sequencer.

Pattern programming

The pattern lane works with blocks of information, not notes. It's a good idea to use the dropdown pattern selector to enter the default pattern for the device, as when you start to insert data it will fill the whole lane with that value until you change it. Setting the snap value to Bar is also a good idea unless you're dealing with unusual pattern changes mid-bar.

Figure 9.15
The Pattern Lane works with blocks of data, not notes

You have to draw data in with the pencil tool. Reason will associate the new data you draw with whichever pattern you select from the menu. Obviously you should only select patterns that contain notes, unless you want the ReDrum to drop out for a few bars, in which case you can select an empty one.

Figure 9.16

Copy, paste and delete pattern change data by drawing around it with the pointer tool and using the familiar Edit menu commands. When pattern selection has been automated in this way, the ReDrum gets a green box around its pattern select buttons.

Here's an interesting way of using Gate CV out from a ReDrum channel to control another device. Take the Gate CV out from a channel on the ReDrum that contains a bass or snare sound. Connect it to the Mono Sequencer Control Gate input on an NN-19, with, say, a piano loaded. Now the drum sound will play a note on the NN-19. Alter the note it plays using the Octave or Semi control on the sampler. This sort of musical trick is used a lot in reggae or hip hop, where a guitar chord might have to play along with a snare beat. Use this method rather than trying to copy and duplicate notes. It ensures that for every drum hit made by that ReDrum channel, the instrument in question will be played too.

Figure 9.17

Making a ReDrum channel trigger a sampler note

Tip

If you connect the Gate output of one ReDrum channel to the Gate in on another, you can play both channels from the same key.

The Dr:Rex Player

REX loops are created by ReCycle, another of Propellerheads' creations. It works by analyzing an audio file and slicing it up into many small parts. The exported REX file can then have its tempo and pitch altered drastically without the side effects that can occur when you timestretch or pitch shift a loop normally. The easiest way to use REX files in Reason is with the Dr:Rex player. Here are some things to know about it.

Working with the Dr:Rex

You can preview REX files from the browser in Reason 3, just like you can with any patch or sound. However you can also load a REX file and audition it without having to place any information on a sequencer track. Just use the Preview button on the Dr:Rex. The loop will automatically adapt to the tempo of your song, regardless of what tempo the loop starts off at.

Figure 10.1
Preview a loop before you place it into the sequencer

The main window on the Dr:Rex provides a good way of editing the slices in a loop before you copy it to the sequencer. Each of the slices can be seen, divided by red lines. You can select any of the slices and the pitch, pan, level and decay controls under the window will alter that particular slice. Let's say you have a drum loop and you want one of the snare hits to be louder and higher. Identify its slice by alt (Mac) or control (PC) clicking on the slice to audition it. Then alter the controls accordingly. Use the Preview button to hear the loop play.

Figure 10.2
You can edit slices independently from the Slice window

You can also move between the slices using the Slice knob. The transpose knob to the left will transpose the entire loop without changing the tempo. This is a good way of matching musical loops to the key of your song. You can use the small keyboard on the window to alter the root key of the loop as well.

Figure 10.3

A REX loop must be copied to its sequencer track before it fully becomes part of the song. However if you play the song and hit the preview button, loops will audition in sync, which helps you see if they're going to work or not. To copy REX notes to the sequencer, press the To Track button on the Dr:Rex. Alternatively, select Edit > Copy REX Loop to Track. In both cases the loop will be copied between the left and right locators regardless of how far apart they are.

Figure 10.4
There are several ways of getting REX data into the sequencer

Tip

To create a large number of instances of a REX loop, rather than copying and pasting, when you press To Track, just make sure the left and right locators are set suitably far apart.

Tip

The Octave and Fine controls can be used to transpose and tune a loop before it is assigned to a sequencer track. Also, if you switch on Select Slice Via MIDI, you can use keyboard keys to automatically select slices in the Dr:Rex.

It is quite possible to play a REX file from the keyboard, treating it essentially as a set of samples. This can be a really interesting way of creating entirely new patterns out of an existing loop. It could be that you love the snare and bass drum sounds in a loop, but don't like the pattern they play. In this case, simply make sure MIDI is directed at the Dr:Rex, then play and record the sequencer while you play the slices in their new pattern from the keyboard. Remember that slices correspond to sequential parts of the loop, not always separate sounds. You may find that the same basic snare sound is triggered from three different keys, or that certain keys

Figure 10.5
Play a REX loop from the keyboard like it was an instrument

trigger slices that contain an entire fill, or a cymbal and a kick drum. This is one of the strengths of re-building loops in this way – you can create some great new patterns with relatively little effort.

Another way of doing this would be to make sure the MIDI notes were in the sequencer, then select them and use Edit > Change Events to introduce some randomization.

Figure 10.6
Use the Change Events option to make Reason create pattern variations for you

Yet another way would be to drag the note data from another instrument's sequencer track to the Dr:Rex's sequencer track. If you do this, remember that the Dr:Rex only responds to as many notes as the loop has slices, so any notes above or below that range won't trigger any sounds. REX files can have over 90 slices, but in practice they don't tend to have more than 20 or 30 maximum.

Figure 10.7
Copy notes from other instruments' tracks to make them play the Dr:Rex

Once notes are in the sequencer there are other ways of messing with them. The most obvious is to enter Edit mode, activate the REX lane or key lane and start to re-arrange notes by hand. Hovering the mouse over the Slice numbers or keys and clicking will audition the slices, and the notes can be edited, lengthened / shortened, moved, duplicated or removed just like any other notes. If you quantize the loop you can impose different timings on it. If you transpose it by transposing the MIDI notes (Edit > Change Events) the pitch won't alter but rather the notes will be shifted up or down the grid, meaning they play back in a totally new pattern.

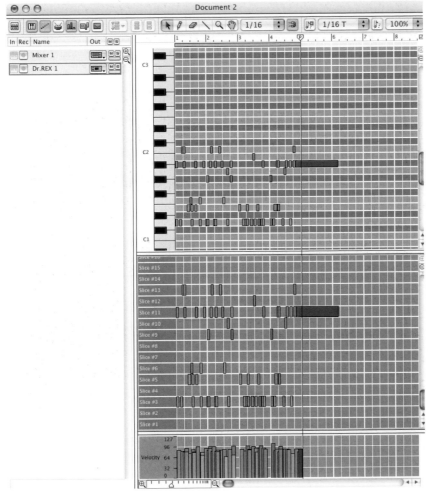

Figure 10.8
Use the REX and Key lanes to manually edit notes. Add, remove or change them

Here are some other tips for how to use REX loops and the REX player.

If you don't want to use drum loops that are obviously sampled, try this. Do the majority of your drum programming in a ReDrum so the patterns are uniquely yours. Then find a REX loop that 'enhances' or backs up the main rhythm. Load it and adjust its volume so that it complements your drums rather than overpowering them. You may have to use the filters on the Dr:Rex to drop most of the bass and some of the mid out of the loop so that it sits behind the main drum rather than competing with it. Also, try using an EQ module to make the REX pattern sit better behind the main drum (Figure 10.9).

Like most of the other instruments, the Dr:Rex has CV ins and outs, and so can be used as a modulation source, or modulated by other sources. Here's an example. Load a Dr:Rex and put a drum loop in it. Copy the notes to the sequencer. Now create a Matrix sequencer with some note data in it and connect its Gate CV out to the Amp Env Gate in on the Dr:Rex. You should get a real cut-up effect on the drums. If you activate Shuffle on the Matrix, you get more of a groove effect (Figure 10.10).

Figure 10.9
Use REX loops as rhythm enhancers rather
than main beats, to avoid an obviously
looped feel to your drums

Figure 10.10
Use a Matrix with CV connected to a Dr:Rex
for cut-up drum effects

Figure 10.11
Connect the Curve out of the Matrix to the OSC Pitch in for some cool filter sweeps

Here's another good way to create some new REX patterns. Load up a Dr:Rex and load a drum or instrument loop. Create a Matrix and enter some data into it. Now connect the Matrix's Note CV out to the OSC Pitch CV input on the Dr:Rex, switching the knob up to full. Spin the rack around and switch the Dr:Rex's octave control all the way to the left. Now, the data you enter in the Matrix will control the pitch of the loop, with some interesting results! Try moving the knob on the OSC pitch input to the centre position for a more trippy sound.

One of the strengths of REX loops is the particular feel that they can have. Even if you don't like a loop's sound, you can still capture its timing. With the REX notes in the sequencer, select a group of notes and right-click (PC) or control+ click (Mac) on them and select Get User Groove. This makes the unique timing of that loop available in the quantize menu for you to apply to other notes. This is really useful for getting a more natural and less mechanical feel to your tracks.

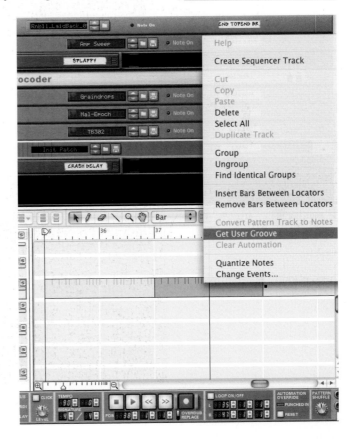

Figure 10.12
Extract the groove from a REX loop and use it to quantize other parts

Tip

Sharpen up your drum loops by moving the decay slider in the Amp section towards the bottom.

A good way of working with sampled loops in the Dr:Rex is to play with the filter section. It's a little predictable, but drum loops do sound good with automated cutoff and filter sweeps! A lot of REX files tend to be in mono, so to increase their stereo width you can switch on the LFO and sync control, choose a waveform and switch the destination to Pan. Remember also to turn up the rate and amount knobs. Get a wah wah effect on the drums by switching the destination to Filter.

Info

A good way of getting control over several REX players at the same time is to put them inside a Combinator. Then you can attach effects, Matrix sequencers and make some unique patterns by drawing in the REX lane for the Combinator and controlling multiple REX players. The results will also only use up a single channel in the main mixer.

Figure 10.14
Put several REX players inside a Combinator. By playing and recording the Combinator, you control all the modules inside it at the same time

The NN-XT Sampler

The NN-XT is a bit like the NN-19, just taken a few steps further, The NN-19 is probably still the best place to quickly load up a sound and start playing. The NN-XT is where you can get more creative with your sampling. What it gives you is a host of synth-like controls for each sample you load in. In the case of a grand piano for example, this means that you can control every single sample that makes up the instrument, independently of every other sample. The rather detailed parameters of the NN-XT's Remote Editor panel are explained in the manual, but here let's look at some of the more useful tricks you can do with this sampler.

Info

The NN-XT can load NN-19 patches and REX loops as well as its own patch format.

Info

In basic mode, you don't need the Remote Editor window open. The basic front panel gives you all the controls you need for simple playback of instruments.

Figure 11.1
In basic use you can run the NN-XT from its front panel, without the Remote Editor open

Here is an interesting way of getting greater control over your REX loops. If you load a REX loop into an NN-XT, it will have its slices mapped over the keys of your keyboard. If you then create a Dr:Rex, load the same loop, copy its notes to the sequencer, move those notes to the NN-XT's track and delete the Dr:Rex, the NN-XT will play back the same pattern as the original REX file. Although it sounds complex this is in fact very quick and easy to achieve. The reason you may want to do it is that you will get the playback of the original loop, but with much greater control over the slices in terms of the way they are played back than you get with a Dr:Rex (Figure 11.2).

Info

Controls on the Remote Editor panel can't be automated.

Figure 11.2
Copy REX notes to the sequencer from a
Dr:Rex then drag to the NN-XT with the same
loop loaded. Result? The same playback but
with greater control over the slices

In The Remote Editor window, each sample you load is displayed down the left.
In the case of multisampled instruments, this generally equates to one sample per
note, and sometimes more than one velocity sample per note. Along the top is the
keyboard. For each sample you can set the key range by clicking and dragging the
handles of the key range, or move it as a single area by picking it up in the middle, or by using the Hi and Lo knobs. You can also drag the scrollbar at the top to
navigate the whole length of the keyboard (Figure 11.3).

Figure 11.3
The Remote Editor shows you which notes are mapped to which keys, and lets you edit these settings

The NN-XT works with zones. Parameters you change for a zone affect the sample inside that zone. Working with zones makes it easier to lay out samples over a keyboard, to layer them up and to move them around.

Figure 11.4
Samples are assigned to zones

You can multiple select samples or zones in the Remote Editor by holding down shift when you select them, or command–clicking (Mac) or control-clicking (PC) on them. A quick way to load a different sample into a zone is to double-click on its name, which opens the browser window (Figure 11.5).

Figure 11.5
Multiple select non-sequential zones to edit several properties at once

The panel of controls along the bottom of the Editor window is contextual, and changes depending on which zone you have selected at that time. However, it's easy to copy parameters between zones. Select the zones you want to copy from and select Edit > Copy Zones, or the same from the contextual menu. Then select the target zones and select Edit > Copy Parameters to Selected Zones.

Figure 11.6
To save time when applying the same settings to different zones, copy and paste using the contextual menu

To layer up several samples into one huge instrument, load all the samples into an NN-XT by using Edit > Add Zone and then simply assign every zone a key range of the whole keyboard. A single key press will now play every sample. This can create some bizarre sounds if the samples are at different speeds and pitches. You can also use the Edit > Duplicate Zone command to create variations on the same sound within an NN-XT. For example, layering up a piano with a filtered version of itself. This sort of thing can be achieved using the Combinator, but if you're just working with samples it's easier with an NN-XT.

Here's a situation you may find yourself in. Imagine you have just loaded up a

Tip

From the browser, if you multiple select a series of samples, the NN-XT will load them all in one go.

group of samples that make up an electric piano. Initially, they are all assigned to the whole keyboard. Not much use. Also, they have rather unhelpful names, so manually setting them up will be a pain. There is an incredibly useful feature that can save you here. With all the samples selected in the NN-XT, choose Edit > Set Root Notes from Pitch Detection. Reason will now work out the pitch of every sample.

Figure 11.7
If you want to create some huge and weird instruments, layer several different samples into one NN-XT and assign them all to the whole keyboard range

Figure 11.8
Reason can work out how groups of samples relate to each other by analysing their pitch

Then, choose Edit > Automap Zones. The NN-XT will order and set the ranges of the samples based on their pitch. In practice, if you have a lot of individual key samples for an instrument, what this does is magically turn the jumble of samples into a fully working and playable instrument on your keyboard. Even after you have done this, you can still add further samples so that, for example, every time you play a certain note on an instrument, you also hear an additional effect. This could be done easily by simply having two zones with the same key range.

Figure 11.9
After Reason has worked out the pitches of multiple samples, use the Automap feature to disperse them over the keyboard, creating a playable instrument. This works best with samples from the same instrument

Tip

Like many other modules, you can audition samples by option-clicking (Mac) or alt-clicking (PC) in the sample column or the keyboard column. If you click in the sample column, you hear the sample unprocessed. If you choose the keyboard column, it plays back with any effects or changes you may have made to it.

Info

Zones can be dragged up or down the list.

If you wanted to graphically separate out certain groups, you can do this by multiple selecting them and choosing Edit > Group Selected Zones. They are then placed together so they become easier to manage. There are several reasons you may want to do this. If you have layered an organ and a synth together, but want to view and edit them more easily, for example. Or, for quickly making settings to groups of zones.

Figure 11.10
Sort samples into groups within an NN-XT to make them easier to manage

It's possible to set up velocity ranges as well as key ranges, so that different zones will play back depending on how hard or soft you play a key. This is commonly used in multisampled, expressive instruments like pianos. On a real piano, when you play the same note at different velocities you get very different sounds. To allow for this in samplers, there are often several samples for the same note, sampled at different velocities. With the addition of velocity crossfading, the overall effect is that when you play a note at different strengths, it changes just like a real instrument. With crossfading switched off, the transition between notes can be very sharp. In some situations this could be desirable, in others, not.

Tip

You could set up an NN-XT so that when you play it softly you get one instrument, but played hard it's a totally different instrument. And of course you can mix and match notes, and make settings with the Lo Vel and Hi Vel knobs.

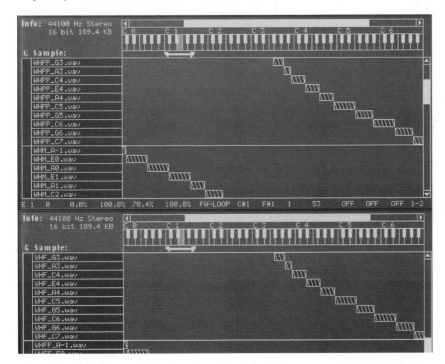

Figure 11.11
In the example of this multisampled piano, there are different samples mapped to the same keys and differentiated by velociy. You can see some samples are called pp (for very soft) and at the other end, ff (for very loud)

Info

Like the NN-19, the two file browser buttons on the NN-XT load different types of sounds. The button on the front panel loads .sxt patches, and the other one loads audio samples.

Tip

The most effective way to alter parameters globally in the Remote Editor is to Select All the samples first.

The NN-XT has 16 audio outputs on its rear panel. These are eight stereo pairs. By default, every zone is routed to the main outputs, 1&2. However you can assign any zone to any of the eight stereo outputs by selecting the zone and using the Out knob under the Editor window to specify a channel.

Figure 11.12
Assign channels out independently for greater flexibility

You will also then have to connect those ports on the back of the sampler to something – most likely a mixer channel. You could use this to process separate zones separately from the rest of the sampler. Used within a combi, you could

Figure 11.13
In this example, some channels are routed separately out of the NN-XT, through some effects, then submixed. The whole thing is contained within a Combinator.

process the zones separately and them join them together again using a Line Mixer, then send the summed stereo output to the main mixer.

It's possible to load multiple .sxt patches into a sampler at the same time! Although a single NN-XT can only load a single patch through its main interface, you can get around it by doing the following. Load two NN-XTs. Into the first one, load your patch. Then select all the zones and choose Edit > Copy Zones. Paste the zones into the second NN-XT, again using the Edit or contextual menus. Then return to the first sampler, load a new patch through the front panel, copy and paste again. Repeat until you have loaded all the .sxt patches you need. This is a quick way of combining several preset sampler patches into a single sampler. Of course you could load all the individual samples, but this is much quicker. You can route the different groups of zones to different outputs to maintain complete level control over them easily in the mixer (Figure 11.14).

Some of the functions of the NN-XT are to an extent duplicated by Reason 3's Remote technology and the Combinator. That is to say, creating key ranges for layered or split multi-instruments, having multiple instruments played from a single MIDI key and processing separate outputs from a multi-instrument. However the functionality is in reality now doubled, as the NN-XT still retains all its features. The possibilities for combining NN-XTs into combis and then having them played by several people at once are astounding.

Tip

Layering sounds gives you many more creative options. Try layering a piano with a gamelan in an NN-XT. It creates a Honky-Tonk piano!

Figure 11.14
Use one NN-XT just to load patches, then copy and paste the zones into a second sampler. Repeat until you have a massive multisampled instrument!

Tip

Use the Start, End and Loop controls for individual zones to tailor each sample. Choose Loop FW-SUS to sustain short sounds.

Tip

Create a sort of arpeggiator effect by looping individual samples and playing with the loop type knob.

Info

The NN-XT's LFO can be set to sync to tempo. This is really useful for creating filter sweeps for chord sounds.

Here's a good way of creating a strange computerized effect with an NN-XT. Load up an acoustic piano. Now connect a Matrix sequencer to the NN-XT. Draw in some notes fairly high up the grid. A fast song tempo helps here too. Then go into curve mode on the Matrix and draw a curve. Connect the Matrix's curve CV out to the OSC Pitch in on the NN-XT. Result when you hit Run on the Matrix? A computer going mad!

Info

The NN-XT has all the usual CV ports round the back, and so can be used as a modulation source / destination for other modules.

Figure 11.15
Create randomized effects by connecting a Matrix to an NN-XT and entering note and curve data

The Subtractor

The Subtractor is a real salt-of-the-earth, no-messing sort of synthesizer. For a detailed description of the principles of subtractive synthesis, as well as the history of monosynths, see the manual and the many online resources. What we're going to look at here is some tips and tricks for getting the most out of the Subtractor in everyday use.

If you're planning on programming your own sounds from scratch it's often a good idea to start with the blank patch that a new Subtractor contains by default. From there you can start to change settings to tailor your sound. The two Oscillator sections form the basis of any sound. By using both oscillators you can get a richer sound. Conversely, by using one you can get a thinner sound, if that's what you're after. For each oscillator you can choose a waveform type. These vary and by mixing and matching them you can create new types of sound. Each oscillator can also be detuned or transposed by octave, which is great for making harmonised sounds or really big sounds.

Figure 12.1
Experiment with the waveforms and oscillator controls to create new sounds

By using the FM control on the oscillator you can create harmonic changes to the sound. By adding a lot of FM to a sound you can drastically change its timbre. Once you have selected a patch, if you click on the patch name field you are presented with a list of all patches within the subfolder you chose. So if you choose a bass sound, a list of all the other bass sounds will be shown (Figure 12.2).

Figure 12.2
Patches can be browsed by group from the patch name window

Some patches – especially basses – default to a polyphony of 1. In certain cases, such as when using acid basses or lead monosynths, it can be desirable to have the synth behave in a monophonic fashion, with only one note playable at once. However, you can increase the polyphony for any sound by simply switching up the polyphony control. This is a good way of getting sound you can't create using real vintage synths. For example, playing bass chords or lead octaves.

Figure 12.3
Increase polyphony to make the Subtractor play polyphonic sounds, even if they start off being monophonic

Tip

To make synth patches sound really big – especially bass patches – try detuning one of the oscillators down an octave. To increase the prominence of lead sounds, tune it up an octave.

You can have a lot of fun with the Subtractor if you automate the controls. This is a good way of simulating the kinds of filter sweeps and hands-on realtime control you get with real synths. In Reason 3, this has particular significance because of the Remote system. By locking controllers to a Subtractor or any other synth, and creating a custom controller map if necessary, you can use the controls in realtime as you play back, even in a live situation. The more realtime controllers you have on your keyboard, the better the control you will have over the instrument.

Figure 12.4
The Subtractor responds particularly well to hands-on control using the Remote system

Tip

If you activate the Ring Mod button and then play with the mix and Phase controls for the two oscillators you can create interesting modifications to your sound.

The filters on the Subtractor are different. The first is multimode and the second is low pass. By enabling the link button you ensure the sound is sent through both, and by automating the filters you can further modify your sounds.

Figure 12.5

The Subtractor is meant in some ways to emulate vintage analogue synthesizers. These synths were traditionally programmed using a step sequencer of some kind. As the Subtractor doesn't have one, you can attach a Matrix sequencer to it to get the same effect. In fact this is often the best way of using a Subtractor, especially for the kinds of electronic sequences that you might want to use in your music. You can program them just using the key editor, but the results will probably sound much better if you use a Matrix (Figure 12.6).

Figure 12.6
Use a Matrix to program believable electronic loops and sequences

Here is a good way of creating a realistic Acid bass sequence.

- Create a Subtractor and load in a bass patch. The TB Synth from the sound bank is a good start. Or you can build your own if you like.
- With the Subtractor selected, create a Matrix sequencer. It will automatically connect its note and gate CV outputs to the Subtractor's Sequencer Control inputs. A resolution of 16 steps is a good starting point for a sequence like this.

Figure 12.7

- Press Run on the Matrix and draw in some note data. Typically, acid bass sequences might contain repeated bass notes with a few variations. It's also a good idea here to drop the octave control on the Matrix so you're writing in bass notes.
- Adjust the pattern until it sounds good to you. Now try turning on osc 2 and playing with its octave control until you get some nice harmonics going.
- Now spin the rack around and connect the Curve CV output from the Matrix to the Filter 1 Freq input on the Subtractor. Go back to the front of the Matrix and switch from Key to Curve mode. Draw in some curve data and hear how the sound takes on a much more acid sweep style (Figure 12.8).
- Try switching the Matrix to Bipolar mode on its rear panel. Now the curve sweep can go to greater extremes, creating an even fatter sweep effect.
- With the Matrix selected in the rack and the sequencer, choose Edit > Copy Pattern to Track, and the note data is placed in the sequencer. If you want you can now delete the Matrix and drag its notes to the Subtractor's sequencer track. However if you do this the curve control that was creating those cool sweeps will disappear. As a Matrix uses very little CPU you may as well leave it in.

Figure 12.8

Figure 12.9
Use both curve and note data from a Matrix to modify and control a Subtractor, for great electronic loops

The Malström

Combining granular and wavetable synthesis into a new form called 'Graintable', the Malström is better suited than the Subtractor to making sharp, pulsating sounds. The basic theory is that the sounds generated by each of the two oscillators are based on graintables, which are a kind of model for generating sound. The best results often come from mixing and matching graintables in both oscillators. It's also rather good at creating sounds that morph and change over time. Here are some tips for working with the Malström.

To select a graintable (i.e. the model used to generate the sound) you can either scroll up and down using the buttons, or click on the name of the graintable and call up a list, grouped by type. You can also deactivate one or both of the oscillators to change the sound. Of course, deactivating both will produce no sound at all!

Figure 13.1
Browse for graintable models from either of the two name fields

Figure 13.2
Small but important, the Legato button can alter the way the Malström responds to your playing

Figure 13.3
There are some useful controls for modifying the playback of each graintable

Figure 13.4
The Mod sections can be synced to the project tempo for some good rhythmic sounds

The Legato button can be used to alter the polyphony of the Malström based on the way you play. With Legato on, if you play a note and then another without releasing the first note, the sound will continue to progress through its envelope rather than starting a new note from the start of the envelope. This is useful if you have a sound with a long duration that changes over time. If you do release one note before you play another, the two sounds will progress independently of one another. This creates a less synced but fuller sound. For free rein, turn off Legato and manually increase or decrease the Polyphony.

Like on the Subtractor, you can use each oscillator's octave and tune controls to make significant changes to the sounds and create bigger effects. Each osc also has Motion, Shift and Index controls. These change the way in which the graintables are played back, and as such can dramatically affect the timbre of the sound. Detailed descriptions are given in the manual, but they are well worth playing around with. One effect they can have if you start to edit them is to send the sound off in different sonic directions as you hold a note.

The next section that affects the sound is the Mod section. Using the curve type selector you can choose what type of modulation is applied to the sound. You can also deactivate one or both modulators. The rate knob determines the resolution at which the modulation is applied and is useful when you activate the sync button for a modulator. This puts it in sync with the song's tempo, and makes it easy to create robotic or arpeggiator effects.

If you select one of the more unusual curve types from higher up the list, the sound will start to take on a 'chopped up' quality in sync with the project. Some good examples of this can be found if you use the patch browser to find some rhythmic Malström patches.

Patch Browser: Malstrom 1

Name	Modified	Size
1FingerFun.xwv	2 Feb 2005 15:56	1 kB
8bitLead.xwv	2 Feb 2005 15:56	1 kB
Arpaweg.xwv	2 Feb 2005 15:56	1 kB
ArpBells.xwv	2 Feb 2005 15:56	1 kB
Arpeggio 2.xwv	2 Feb 2005 15:56	1 kB
Arpeggio 3.xwv	2 Feb 2005 15:56	1 kB
Arpichoke.xwv	2 Feb 2005 15:56	1 kB
Arpobahn (hold).xwv	2 Feb 2005 15:56	1 kB
Band Oscillations.xwv	2 Feb 2005 15:56	1 kB
Comb.xwv	2 Feb 2005 15:56	1 kB
Culpa Arpi.xwv	2 Feb 2005 15:56	1 kB
Cycling9s.xwv	2 Feb 2005 15:56	1 kB
Cygnus.xwv	2 Feb 2005 15:56	1 kB
Eau de Neon.xwv	2 Feb 2005 15:56	1 kB
FlangedFun.xwv	2 Feb 2005 15:56	1 kB
Fooled Again.xwv	2 Feb 2005 15:56	1 kB

Figure 13.5

Because of the two distinct sound generators you can get sounds that appear to be made up of multiple parts. For example, locate the patch called Arpobahn. Press a key and you'll hear two parts to the sound. If you deactivate osc B you'll be left just with the thumping sound. If you reactivate osc B and switch off osc A, you're left only with the synth lead sounds. This patch also has a lot of portamento applied, which makes for interesting sweeps in pitch as you move around the keyboard.

Figure 13.6
Having two sound generation sections means you can create patches with distinctly different elements to them

Around the back

The Malström has more types of connection on its rear panel than most other instruments in Reason. For example, you can bypass the filter section entirely by sending the Osc A and B audio outputs to the mixer rather than the main stereo outs.

Figure 13.8
Send the Osc outputs rather than main outputs to the mixer

The Sequencer control CV inputs lets you play the Malström from a Matrix or a ReDrum, and works best with monophonic sounds.

Figure 13.9
The Malström responds well to Matrix control, especially for making sequences

Interestingly there's also an audio input on the Malström. Sadly not for recording audio, but for sending external sources to the filters. If you connect an audio output from another device you can process it through the filters or shaper of the Malström. It will then be mixed with the sound being generated by the oscillators and collectively sent to the output.

Figure 13.10
Process the audio output of any instrument through the Malström's filters

There are other interesting routing options, like the ability to place an external effect device between the oscillators and the filters on a Malström. You would connect an osc output to the input on the effect device, and the effect's output back to the audio input on the Malström.

Figure 13.11
Some interesting routing using the ins and outs on the Malström

The effect devices

E ffect devices don't generate sound, they modify it. Part of Reason's flexibility lies in the fact that as well as having multi-functional instruments and a sequencer, it also has many different types of effect device to colour your sounds and add depth to them. It's fairly essential to use effects of some kind on your tracks. They all have very different uses but the most common are reverb, delay, compression and distortion. There are a couple of things to say about the general use of effects. The first is that if you're making more conventional music, less is often more when it comes to effects. Using them sparingly can often be a lot more effective than applying them in great swathes. Conversely, if you are being more experimental, over-using effects can be a great way to get some really unique sounds. Here are some common features of all the effect devices in Reason.

Effect devices are created in the same way as instruments, by selecting Edit > Create or right-clicking in the rack and choosing a device. They can also be deleted in the same way as instruments. They are patched using cables, and can be renamed by clicking their name field to make it editable.

Tip

When an effect has signal playing through it, the LED meter on its left will light up. You can bypass or mute an effect without actually deleting it by using the control on the top left corner.

Tip

If you have edited (i.e. moved) knobs on an effect device you can quickly reset them to their default position by command-clicking (Mac) or control-clicking (PC) on them.

Figure 14.1
Create effect devices from the Create menu or the contextual menu

Different effects all impose varying amounts of drain on your CPU. The smaller effects like the Phaser or RV7 reverb create relatively little strain. Some of the RV7000 or MClass patches by comparison are pretty heavy.

Effects can be freely routed just like instruments. With the new Combinator in Reason 3, you can create complex effects chains within a Combi and then save it as a combi patch. Then when you need it again, just call up the single patch rather than re-building it all from scratch. This can save a huge amount of time copying and pasting or using template files.

Figure 14.2

An example of a complex effect module built inside a Combinator. This can be saved and loaded very quickly

Most of the parameters on effects units can be controlled in realtime. In Reason 3 with the new Remote system this means that you can map individual controllers to, say, effect type selectors, depth amounts or delay resolutions, and change them

Figure 14.3
Using Remote to control a Reverb unit in realtime from the keyboard

---

Info

Some of the effect devices have CV (Control Voltage) inputs which can be used creatively to receive CV signal from instruments to modulate their output in unusual ways.

---

while you play. This can give your music a much more organic feel. To achieve the same thing in a studio setting, they can of course be automated in the usual way.

Insert or Send?

Effects are applied in one of two ways – inserts or sends. To create a send effect, select a main mixer (ReMix), a chained mixer or a smaller line mixer and then create the effect. It will automatically be routed as a send effect through the mixer's aux bus. To create an insert effect, select any instrument module in the rack and create the effect. Wiring is then automatically done so that the instrument's outputs are routed through the effect and then on to the mixer. You can create any number of insert effects as a chain attached to an instrument, or as many as your computer can handle, at least.

Figure 14.4
Create an effect whilst an instrument is selected and the effect is applied as an insert, between the instrument and the mixer

When effects are used as inserts, a signal chain is in force. That is, the signal is passed through the effects in a hierarchical way, top to bottom (unless you manually rewire them). With sends, you determine how much of the 'wet' (effected) signal is mixed with the 'dry' signal.

Figure 14.5
Some effects attached to the main mixer as sends

Which effect to choose?

The kinds of effects you might use on most channels – say, reverb, compression and delay, are best to attach to the mixer as sends. If every channel needs a little reverb, rather than attaching a reverb unit to each instrument at great cost to your CPU, attach one to the mixer as a send and then just send differing amounts of

Figure 14.6
Frequently used effects work best attached to the mixer as sends.

each channel to it using the aux sends on the mixer. You will only be able to use one preset on the reverb unit, but there's nothing to stop you using more than one of the same type of effect as a send (Figure 14.6).

Creating chains of insert effects is a great way of messing with a sound before it even gets to the mixer. By using the Combinator to do this, chains are easier to manage and also can be stored as Combi patches for instant recall.

When you use inserts, the order of the effects units changes the sound. For example, if you have a distortion, then an EQ, then a reverb you will get a certain sound. If you move a device or add another one into the chain somewhere you may find the behaviour of devices further along the chain changes as they process the different sound. For example, if you apply an EQ that takes out the high frequencies of a sound, the delay that comes next in the chain may suddenly become much less pronounced. These sorts of changes are very specific to the kinds of sounds and effects you work with, so it's hard to come up with any definite rules. One thing that is for sure is that by combining effects in chains you can create unique sounds that you can't get with any one single effect.

Figure 14.7
By creating a chain of inserts on an instrument you can build unique effects

Scream 4

The Scream 4 is much more than just a distortion unit. It lets you add all kinds of warmth, crunch or overdrive to your sounds. One side effect of using digital music sequencers is that the signal they produce can sound overly clean and lacking in bite. Almost every type of sound – synths, basses, drums, pads – can benefit from some warming up using a Scream 4. Unlike most of the other effects units it can store and load its own patches, with the suffix .SM4. This makes it easy to save and recall your favourite Scream effects. Here are some tips for using the Scream 4.

The Damage section has ten basic types of distortion available, and each has two controls which alter different parameters depending on the type of damage you choose. There are no hard rules about what type to use for what – in fact the most interesting results can come when you're trying things that you may not at first think will work. However, the ten types of effect do have certain real-world counterparts.

Figure 14.8

- Overdrive is typical of the sound produced by analogue amps when they're pushed right to the limit. Used subtly it adds 'edge' to sounds without making them jump out of the mix.
- Distortion is a bit more in-your-face than Overdrive, and better for heavier crunch effects.
- Fuzz is more of an angry, 1960s guitar type of effect.
- Tube distortion is warmer and more dense than other types.
- Tape is an interesting one because it recreates the kind of artefacting typical of magnetic tape saturation. Used properly it can make sound much more lifelike and less digital-sounding. It can be a good idea to apply this to the entire mix, by inserting it between the mixer and the hardware interface.
- Feedback feeds your sound back into itself, producing some strange results.
- Modulate blends the signal with a compressed, filtered version of itself, resulting in resonant distortion effects.
- Warp is particularly nasty and produces a high, mangled sound.
- Digital emulates the low bit resolutions of early digital equipment. Bit reduction is a particularly unique kind of digital sound. The lower the resolution and rate, the more chopped-up the sound. Great for vintage arcade game types of effect.
- Scream adds a bandpass filter before the distortion stage. Use the two control knobs to control its frequency. By moving the P2 knob you can get some good wah-wah effects.

The Cut section can be used to fine tune the effect, boosting or cutting the lo, mid and hi frequency bands.

The Body section simulates types of acoustic space in which your sound is effected. Some presets correspond to a type of speaker cabinet and others are unique to the Scream 4. By experimenting with these settings you can further tweak your sound.

Figure 14.9

One of the Scream 4's more hidden features is its CV controls. On the rear panel are four CV ins and one CV out. By connecting CV outs from instruments to these inputs you can control the amount of damage effect, the two P knobs and the Scale parameter. Here is an example. Create a Dr.Rex player and load a drum loop. Then connect a Scream 4 to it. Go to the rear panel and connect the Mod Output from the Dr.Rex to the Damage Control input on the Scream 4. The result is a much more chopped-up drum sound with much harder attack.

Figure 14.10

Try switching the cable to the LFO output on the Dr.Rex. The effect is a kind of reverse drum loop.

Figure 14.11

In another example, create a ReDrum and play a drum loop into the sequencer. Attach a Scream 4 as an insert and route the Auto CV output from the Scream 4 to the Pitch CV in on one of the active drum channels. The pitch of that drum hit is now actively modulated by the Scream 4. There are more uses for the Auto CV out. For example, by sending Auto CV through a Spider unit and inverting the signal you can achieve 'ducking' effects, whereby increasing the volume of one sound source will decrease the volume of the other.

Figure 14.12
Modulate individual drum channels using the Scream 4

For modules that have individual outputs for each of their channels like the ReDrum or NN-XT, it's quite possible to process only specific channels through the Scream 4, or any other effect module. Simply manually patch the relevant channel through the effect. In this way you could for example process the snare and bass sounds through an effect, but leave the cymbals clean and running to the mixer. In this situation, using the Spider Audio merger / splitter is useful (Figure 14.13).

As the Scream 4 has different sections, you can activate only the ones you want. For example, by only using the Body section you can create specific sonic effects related to the quality of a sound without applying any distortion at all. To create wah-wah effects, connect an instrument's LFO CV out to the Scale CV in on the Scream 4 and play with the controls until you get the effect you want.

Figure 14.13
In this example, several drum channels are sent to a Spider audio merger, then through the Scream 4, then grouped and sent to the mixer. The remaining drum channels go straight to the mixer as usual

RV7000

Reverb is one of those curious effects that, if it does its job properly, you shouldn't notice unless it's turned off. What reverb does is effectively make things sound further away, so it should be used with care, unless that's the effect you're particularly going for. A good trick is to use a very small amount of short reverb on most channels. Although you can use a reverb as a send effect and apply a little to each channel in the mixer, remember too that software allows you to insert as many as you want throughout the rack. Different types of reverb work better with different sounds. Strings, for example, benefit from lush, warm reverbs. Drums sound good through short, snappy reverbs.

The RV7000 has a good selection of presets, and like the Scream 4 it can store and load patches. To get into more detailed editing of the reverb, open the Remote Programmer by clicking on the socket to the bottom left of the unit. Now, by using the three buttons on the left of the programmer you can access the three types of parameter – reverb, EQ and gate.

Figure 14.14
The RV7000's remote programmer allows detailed reverb editing

In the Reverb section of the programmer, use the eight knobs to control all the parameters of the reverb. The most useful are Algorithm, which switches between basic reverb types, Tempo Sync (where applicable) and Diffusion. The Dry / Wet control on the main panel controls the overall amount of effect applied. You can get some really cool dub-style delay effects by using the reverse, multi tap, echo and spring algorithms. For more cinematic reverbs, try the FilmScore preset. Remember that you can chain these units together to create multi-layered effects.

Figure 14.15
Create effects chains of reverbs with varied dry / wet amounts to create that perfect effect

By using the EQ controls on the RV7000 you can shape the character of the reverb, not the original sound. If you are mixing wet and dry versions of the same sound you may need to drop out certain frequency bands in the wet signal.

Additional effects units

The smaller effects modules are more straightforward and very simple to operate. Here are a few tips for using them.

- The RV-7 reverb is a good alternative to the RV7000 if CPU power is a problem. Interesting presets include Stereo Echoes and Low Density.
- The DDL-1 delay can be set to delay in different units. Switch between them to get different styles of delay. In Steps mode the delay will always sync to tempo. In MS mode, the delay operates freely.

Figure 14.16

- The D-11 Distortion is a no-frills alternative to the Scream 4.
- The ECF-42 filter can be used as a regular filter but you can also route CV or MIDI from a program device or the sequencer to create pattern-controlled filter effects.
- The CF-101 unit adds chorus or flanging to a sound, and can be used to create richer textures.

- The PF-90 phaser adds sweeping effects, ideal for guitar and vocal sounds.
- The UN-16 Unison works by adding a sort of chorus, and gives the effect of a wider, fuller sound.
- The COMP-01 compressor evens out the loudest and softest parts of a sound, increasing the overall volume. Basses and drums particularly benefit from compression. Use heavier compression for a 'pumped' effect.
- The PEQ-2 lets you precisely boost or cut frequencies in the sound that is processed through it.
- The Spider Audio Merger / Splitter can either take several audio signals and merge them into a single output, or take a single source and split it up to four ways. There are several uses for this. You could for example use it to sub-group a number of modules. Or, by splitting, you could send one signal through several effects units and into separate mixer channels, which saves time and power by ensuring you don't have to start duplicating devices or sequencer tracks.

Figure 14.17
Use the Spider to merge or split audio for many different purposes

- The Spider CV Merger / Splitter can either merge four CV sources into one, or split one into four. You could for example use one Matrix device to control several instruments, or have several instruments modulating a single unit.

The MClass effects

New in Reason 3, the MClass suite of mastering effects helps to bring a more professional sound to your Reason tracks by adding various processing modules to the signal chain. Good mastering gives music greater depth, punch and clarity, as well as ensuring a good overall level of gain. Like mixing, it depends on the track, the monitors you listen to it on, your ears and the room you listen in. There is a lot of good information available out there on how to master, but let's look at a few of the MClass's tricks.

The MClass effects are available separately or as a combi, and can be applied individually to any instrument, and used as many times in a rack as your CPU can handle. When you are using an MClass Combi for mastering, attach it between the mixer and the Hardware Interface. This will ensure that the whole signal passes through it. Make sure you select the Hardware Interface and then create the Combi.

Figure 14.18
A Mastering combi sits well at the very final audio output stage of Reason

A Combi is the best way of using the MClass effects specifically for mastering. Click on the name field and you can select from a list of presets with sensible names like Dance, Hard Rock and so on. Don't be afraid to try a preset that you may expect not to suit your music. It could be that the Drum and Bass preset works really well on an acoustic track – you never know until you try.

Figure 14.19
The Factory Sound Bank has some good mastering combi patches to get you started

You can tweak any of the presets, or build your own mastering combi by creating a Combinator and filling it with any of the effect modules. You can of course mix the MClass and other effects to get unique sounding effects chains.

The MClass effects are equally adept when used individually, as insert or send effects. Here is a look at what they do.

MClass Equalizer

The has two bands and high and low shelving bands. You can use the Lo Cut switch as a sort of 'rumble reducer', as it removes all frequencies below 30HZ. EQ can help to make sounds sit properly in the mix and blend together. It may be that you EQ a guitar, for example, to sit well in a mix. It doesn't matter that by itself it might sound thin, as long as it works in the track. If you are using your own samples you may need to roll off some of the top end, if any of them have hiss recorded on them.

MClass Stereo Imager

The MClass Stereo Imager addresses one of the more long-standing issues with Reason's mixdowns – the lack of real stereo width. Splitting the signal into Lo and Hi frequency bands, you can widen out the higher frequencies whilst narrowing the lower ones. The result of this is that the top end gets opened out while the bottom end is pulled in and made tighter. You can process the separate bands separately by manually re-patching on the rear panel.

MClass Compressor

The MClass Compressor features a Soft Knee mode to give you a more gentle compression and reduce the undesirable 'pumping' effect that can result from harsh compression. It also has sidechain inputs, which allow you to use an audio signal to trigger the compressor. You can use this to create the so-called 'ducking' effect, whereby when one sound plays it will dramatically reduce the volume of another.

MClass Maximizer

The MClass Maximizer tackles the problem of quiet mixes by limiting. It increases the overall perceived loudness of a mix without ever distorting or clipping. Use a combination of Soft Clipping and boosting the output gain to make a mix louder without it sounding too pumped or hitting the red. This can be particularly useful

---

Figure 14.20
Use the Lo Cut switch as a sort of 'rumble reducer'

Figure 14.21
The MClass Stereo Imager improves stereo width

Figure 14.22
The MClass Compressor features a Soft Knee mode to give you a more gentle compression

Figure 14.23
The Maximizer increases overall perceived volume

Figure 14.23
The Maximizer increases overall perceived volume

to use as an insert if you have imported your own samples into a sampler and they are too quiet. Rather than pushing faders to the max, use a Maximizer.

The use of mastering effects is a very personal process. Some people prefer less, some more. But what is true is that they make quite a difference to the overall sound quality of your mixes. To see just how much, try switching them off and hear the life and energy instantly drop out of your track.

BV512 Vocoder

Vocoding is a fairly familiar effect these days – the process of taking a sound and making it robotic, or synth-like. Some of the interesting uses for the vocoder involve moving away from the more obvious applications and instead vocoding other sounds like drums or guitars for special effects. Here are a couple of things to remember about the Vocoder.

It's a little more complex than the other effects, in that it requires two types of input to work. A carrier signal (typically a pad or string patch) and a modulator signal (typically speech or vocals). The Vocoder looks at the frequency characteristics of the modulator signal and applies them to the carrier, outputting the result. Essentially, the speech is 'playing' the synth. The speech sample isn't being effected as such, but rather its characteristics are being used to modulate another sound. The reason it works best with pads or strings is that they have a constant quality to them. You can use any sound, but with sounds that are already rhythmic, the effect of the vocoding is much less apparent.

As Reason doesn't record audio directly in, you can't sing straight through a Vocoder. Instead, use the NN-19, ReDrum, REX or NN-XT modules to load pre-recorded samples that you have created in another program. One of the advantages of loading lots of samples into, say, a ReDrum is that you can have them all running through a single Vocoder, which will save you power and space in the rack.

Figure 14.24
The BV512 Vocoder is a little more complex than the other effects

The more filter bands you use on a Vocoder, the more accurately the output will match the characteristics of the modulator signal. By using the Band control you can toggle between band settings. The setting you use will depend on your desired effect, as a more lo-fi effect can be achieved by using fewer bands. Alternatively, if you select the FFT setting you will get the most accurate voice vocoding setting. This essentially simulates 512 frequency bands, hence the name of the module. It's best to use FFT for vocoding vocals, not instruments.

Figure 14.25
Choose a Band setting that suits the type of
effect you need

A full guide to setting up the Vocoder can be found in the manual. However, here are some useful tips for using it in day-to-day situations, and some possible applications for it.

- Carrier devices should ideally be bright, synth or string-like patches. This is because the more signal there is, the more the Vocoder has to play with and so the better the eventual output. They also tend to sustain indefinitely rather than tailing off, which is helpful in this case.
- A Subtractor or Malström can be used as a carrier with the just the Init patch loaded. Make a few tweaks to the detune knobs, and off you go.
- If you assign MIDI to the Vocoder's sequencer channel (assuming you have created one) you can 'play' the individual bands using MIDI keys.
- The band level controls on the Vocoder can be automated, with a separate subtrack for each band. You must have first created a sequencer track for the Vocoder before any automation can take place.

Figure 14.26
Automating the bands on a vocoder

Figure 14.27
Using a Spider to creatively modulate signal through a vocoder

- By using a rhythmic loop – say, a REX drum loop – as the modulator source, you can effectively arpeggiate the carrier signal. Basically this means that when you play, whatever is loaded into the carrier module plays rhythmically based on the sound of the REX loop. If you duplicate the Dr. Rex player in the rack, you can have synths and drum loops playing the same rhythm, which sounds great.
- To get a more precise rhythmic modulation you can of course program your own beats in a ReDrum and use that as a modulator signal.

The Vocoder has comprehensive CV in and out on the rear panel, which means you can get very creative with using it both as a source and a destination for modulating other devices, or using others to modulate individual bands. They can also be cross-patched if you're feeling really adventurous.

You can use a single device both as a carrier and a modulator, with interesting results. Use a Spider Audio splitter to send audio from a device to both sets of inputs on the Vocoder. If you do, it's worth adding an EQ or a distortion module between the Spider and the Vocoder to give it a bit more punch. This works well with drums, giving a heavily filtered effect.

The Hold button will freeze the current state of the Vocoder and the sound won't change until you click it again. This is good for playing live as it gives you more control over how the sound plays. Again, the button can be controlled from a MIDI keyboard using Remote or Keyboard Control modes, leaving you free from the mouse to concentrate on playing.

Figure 14.28
Freeze the state of the vocoder with the Hold button

Exporting from Reason

S o you've spent ages on building and automating your tracks, and now it's time to export them so you can put them on CD and play them to the world. There are two ways in which you can do this – by recording the track to a realtime media like a CD recorder, DAT or MiniDisc, or by exporting it to an audio file. The latter is by far the most common with Reason, but here's a quick description of how you might do it using the first method.

Exporting in realtime

This used to be the accepted way of mixing down before computers became so commonplace. Basically it just means playing the track out in realtime and recording it to some kind of magnetic or optical media like a tape or CD. It is a perfectly acceptable way of mixing down, although in reality, now that every computer has a CD burner, and you're more likely to want to upload mp3s of your work, it often makes sense to export straight to computer's hard drive. One case in which you would almost certainly need to record out to DAT or CD in realtime is if you have routed Reason's tracks out directly through your audio interface by manually patch-

Figure 15.1
If you are routing audio from Reason out through your soundcard's separate outputs, realtime mixdown may well be the way to go

ing channels through the Hardware Interface. In this situation you may well be processing Reason's tracks through external hardware effects and a mixer, and those effects would only be recorded if the total summed output of Reason (main stereo outs plus any separated channels) were all collected together and recorded on a single device.

Mixdown is a good time to apply a fade in or fade out to your track. This is done by automating the master fader. As you record, move the fader smoothly up or down. Alternatively, open the automation subtrack for the master fader by alt or control-clicking on it. Then draw automation in with the pen tool or, better still, with the line tool to create a smooth ramp. Remember that to automate anything on the mixer you must first create a sequencer track for it.

Figure 15.2
Automate the master fader for a smooth fade out

A note about ReWire

If you are running Reason in ReWire mode with Sonar, Cubase, Logic or any other compatible program, Reason's audio outs are inextricably linked with that program. The export options in Reason will be greyed out as they can't operate independently of the host program. In this case, selecting audio mixdown in the host program will include Reason's output in its mixdown, meaning you don't have to worry about it.

Figure 15.3
In ReWire mode, Reason's export options are transferred to the host program, such as Cubase

Checking everything

There are some tips for actually mixing your music in the chapter on the Mixer, which all apply here. After you have perfected the levels and the automation for your track, make sure the left and right markers are positioned over the start and finish of your track. Leave at least one bar of empty space either side. If your track ends with an echoing sound of any kind, make sure to leave a few bars of space, or it will be cut off. If you need more space on the timeline, drag the E marker further to the right.

Tip

Zoom out so you can see your entire track graphically on the timeline. This will help you check if the markers are in the right place.

Figure 15.4
If you need more space, drag the End marker to the right

Make sure everything that should be unmuted is unmuted. Select File > Export Song as Audio File. Choose somewhere sensible to put it. If you're on a Mac, choose the AIFF format. On a PC, choose WAVE. For audio CD you'll want to select a sample rate of 44.1kHz and a bit depth of 16 bit.

Figure 15.5
Choose an audio output format depending on your platform of choice

As a rule of thumb, don't go above or below these settings unless you know why you need to. Most video editing programs run at 48KHz but can happily deal with audio sampled at 44.1. If you are exporting to 16 bits you can tick the Dither box, which will make sure there's no distortion introduced by changing bit depths. Reason now renders down your track, including all the effects and automation, to a single file. If the track is long and has lots of effects and instruments, this might take a moment or two.

Figure 15.6
The Dither option in Reason 3 ensures clean bit rate conversion

If for some reason you need every track as an individual file, for remixing purposes, you can simply solo up one track at a time and export it. This is a bit time-intensive, and is better achieved by using ReWire to record tracks simultaneously through into a host sequencer, if you have the software.

If you haven't already inserted one, it's a good idea to put an MClass mastering Combi between the mixer and the Hardware Interface and select or modify a preset that suits your music best. The changes to the sound introduced by the MClass effects are included in the mixdown. You'll be surprised by how much bigger and wider it can make your track sound.

Figure 15.7
Introduce a mastering combi between the Mixer and the Hardware Interface to improve the overall sound of a mix

There are some other export options worth mentioning.

- Export MIDI File will export the entire track as a MIDI file, ideal for sharing over the internet or for backing up.

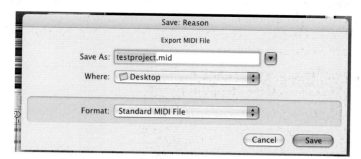

Figure 15.8

- Export Device Patch will export the current patch of whichever device you have selected. This is really just another way of performing the save function from the front of the modules.
- Export REX as MIDI File will create a file containing just the MIDI data contained in a REX loop, not the audio.
- Export Loop as Audio File is especially useful if you are taking small sections of music into other programs to work with. For instance, if you have a great drum loop, you probably only need four bars of it to take into Pro Tools to do a remix. Or, for multimedia purposes where small loops are necessary for quick download speeds, taking a bit of something is easier than taking it all. Remember when you do any kind of export from Reason that what gets exported is what's audible. That is, if you don't want certain tracks to be present in the exported audio file, you have to mute them. Anything that's muted will be left out.

If you are working on different machines, remember that you must have the same sets of sounds present on all machines for projects to play back properly. You can use the Search and Proceed warning box that pops up to find the files, but only if they're on the system somewhere. If you are using lots of your own samples and moving around it's a good idea to use the ReFill Packer that comes with Reason to organize them into ReFills, which are easy to manage.

Sharing and publishing

Figure 15.9
Use the supplied ReFill packer to organize and share your samples and patches in ReFill format

If you choose to upload your songs to the web or send them to anyone, there are steps you can take to ensure your work is identified as your own. Here are some tips for publishing songs.

If you choose File > Song Self-Contain Settings, you can see exactly what parts of what ReFills you are using in your track. This window displays audio files, not patches. Remember that Reason project files are just instructions – they don't include any audio data. For this reason, you have to make sure that if you are sending someone the file as a Reason project rather than an mp3, you must also include any relevant ReFills. Otherwise, when they open it they will just be prompted to locate the missing files. Projects will still open, but any missing files will be replaced by silence.

Figure 15.10

By selecting File > Song Information you can embed data about yourself and your music. You can select a 256x256 pixel image, enter your URL and email and some text of you like. If you choose to show the Splash window on open, it will always pop up when the song is loaded (Figure 15.11).

Regular Reason project files can be modified by whoever opens them. However, if you don't want anyone to be able to mess with your work, choose File > Publish Song. What you then create is an .rps file which can be opened and edited but not saved. Also, if the song is edited in any way, it cannot be exported as audio until it has been quit and re-opened in its original form. This means that it's impossible (or at least very hard) for anyone to remix your track or change it without your per-

Figure 15.11
Embed text, URL and email information and
your choice of picture in your song file

mission. Interestingly, the option to export patches is also greyed out in .rps files, meaning that if you have created a killer synth sound, nobody can steal it – unless you want them to!

Figure 15.12
A published Reason song is relatively well
protected against changes or borrowing of
patches

On the whole there are no cross-platform issues between Reason on a PC or Mac. A Reason file is just a Reason file, and that's that. As there are no plugins to deal with, that's not a problem either. The only possible incompatibility is if you have some audio files on one system but not another. Be aware also that you can't open files made in a newer version of Reason in an older version of the software. If you are working in Version 3, stick with it. If you're working in version 2.5, don't start working in version 3 unless you are prepared to switch permanently.

Index